رفقا أهل السنة بأهل السنة

RIFQAN AHLUS SUNNAH BI AHLUS SUNNAH

GENTLENESS

O PEOPLE OF THE SUNNAH, WITH THE PEOPLE OF THE SUNNAH

SHAYKH 'ABDUL-MUHSIN AL-ABBAD

REVISED 2ND EDITION

DAR AL-ARQAM

ISBN 0 9928136 0 4

British Library Cataloguing in Publishing Data.
A catalogue record for this book is available from the British Library

Published by:
Dar Al-Arqam Publishing
W: www.daral-arqam.co.uk
E: info@daral-arqam.co.uk
E: daralarqam@hotmail.co.uk

Cover design & typeset by:
Azhar Majothi @ www.ihsaandesign.com

Edited by Adnan ibn Fazal Karim

Many thanks to the Quran & Sunnah Society of Canada for allowing the use of their original translation.

Contents

بسم الله الرحمن الرحيم

Translator's Foreword

The praise is for Allah. We praise Him, we seek aid from Him, and we seek forgiveness from Him. We seek refuge with Allah from the evils of our souls and the misdeeds of our deeds. Whoever Allah guides, then there is no misguider for him and whoever He leaves astray, then there is no guide for him.

I testify that there is no god worthy of worship except Allah alone. He has no partner. And I testify that Muḥammad is His servant and His Messenger.

As for what follows, then indeed the truest of speech is the Book of Allah and the best guidance is the guidance of Muḥammad ﷺ. The evilest of affairs are their innovations. Every innovation is a heresy, every heresy is misguidance, and all misguidance is in the Fire.

The treatise before you is a translation of the second edition of the highly beneficial advice titled, *Rifqan Ahl as-Sunnah bi Ahl as-Sunnah,*[1] written by the noble shaikh, Abū 'Abdir-Razzâq 'Abdul-Muḥsin bin Ḥamad al-'Abbâd al-Badr. Though I first published this translation of mine online in 2008, the book is

---

[1] **[t]** al-Badr, 'Abdul-Muḥsin bin Ḥamad. *Rifqan Ahl as-Sunnah bi Ahl as-Sunnah* (2nd ed). Riyâḍ, 1426H.

still very relevant today. The treatise, first written by the shaikh in 2003/1424H, was originally written as a much needed and timely advice directed to his brothers and sisters among the People of the Sunnah due to the turmoil and controversy that had occurred as a result of the defamation and heretication of certain scholars like Shaikhs 'Adnân 'Ar'ūr, Muḥammad al-Maghrâwî, and Abul-Ḥasan al-Ma'ribî.[2] In the second edition, which was published in 2005/1426H—a mere two years later—the shaikh added a new introduction addressing some issues that were raised when the first edition was published and distributed. He also added the last two chapters of his follow up treatise to *Rifqan Ahl as-Sunnah*, titled *al-Ḥathth 'alâ Ittibâ' as-Sunnah wat-Taḥdhîr min al-Bida' wa Bayân Khaṭarihâ*, to the end of it.

In this translation of mine, I have tried to stay as true to the original Arabic text as I could, adding certain things in brackets [ ] to facilitate an understanding of what is being said. I have provided references to the Qur'anic verses quoted by the shaikh, as he normally does not give the references for them in his works. I have also added my own footnotes throughout to aid the reader with understanding certain terms, expressions, or references used by the shaikh. I have indicated these footnotes prefixing them with the symbol **[t]**. In cases where a footnote includes comments both from myself as well as from the shaikh, I have distinguished his comments with the symbol **[a]**; all other footnotes throughout this work belong to the shaikh, may Allah

---

[2] **[t]** This treatise was first published during the height of the turmoil surrounding al-Ma'ribî, who had been made a pariah for his refusal to toe the line with respect to the defamation and heretication of other scholars from Ahl as-Sunnah (i.e., 'Adnân 'Ar'ūr and Muḥammad al-Maghrâwî). He became (and remains to be) the litmus test for one's Salafism: hereticate him and you pass, defend him and you fail.

preserve and protect him. All references made throughout the book refer to the original Arabic works.

At the end of the work before you, I have also included another follow up treatise that the shaikh wrote in December 2010/Muḥarram 1432H) titled, *Marrah Ukhrâ: Rifqan Ahl as-Sunnah bi Ahl as-Sunnah*, which shows just how relevant the original advice still is this current day.

Aboo Ishaaq Rasheed Gonzales
Toronto, Ontario, Canada
QSS Canada
Friday, January 5, 2014/Rabî' al-Awwal 4, 1435H

بسم الله الرحمن الرحيم

Introduction to the Second Edition[3]

The praise is for Allah. May Allah send salutations, peace, and blessing upon our Prophet Muḥammad, upon his family, his Companions and whoever was a supporter of his, held to his sunnah, and was guided by his guidance, until the Day of Reward.[4]

As for what follows, then a few years prior (after the death of our venerable shaikh,[5] Shaikh of Islam 'Abdul-'Azîz bin 'Abdillah bin Bâz, in 1420H and the death of the shaikh, 'Allâmah[6] Muḥammad bin Ṣâliḥ bin 'Uthaimîn, in 1421H ﷭), division and separation occurred between some of the People of the Sunnah. It resulted from some of them undertaking the pursuit of errors

---

[3] **[t]** This heading is not found in the original text and was added to distinguish between the first and second introductions to the book.

[4] **[t]** Ar. yawm ad-dîn (يَوم الدين) – lit. the Day of Reward (also Ar. yawm al-jazâ' (يَوم الجزاء)). See *al-Qâmūs al-Muḥîṭ*. It refers to Judgement day, which is also referred to as the Last Day (Ar. yawm al-âkhir (يَوم الآخر)) and the Day of Standing (Ar. yawm al-qiyâmah (يَوم القيامة)); the day when all of mankind will stand before their Lord to be judged.

[5] **[t]** Ar. shaikh (شَيخ) – elder, chief. It is an honorific given to religious scholars, teachers and elders.

[6] **[t]** Ar. 'allâmah (عَلَّامة) – great scholar, extremely learned. It is an honorific given to scholars of vast knowledge.

[by] some of their brothers from the People of the Sunnah then cautioning against them,[7] while those they incriminated countered their speech with its like. The spreading of this division's tribulation was assisted by the ease of obtaining these incriminations, cautionings, and what countered them, from internet information (in which all [those] whose slander was desired were slandered at any time of the night or day). So all of those who desired it seized it and because of that, the rift of the division and separation was widened and everyone took sides with whomever and whatever delighted them from the individuals and the speech. The matter did not stop with the incrimination of whoever was incriminated from the People of the Sunnah. Rather, that passed on to some of those who did not support that incrimination. In the beginning of 1424H, I wrote a treatise of advice regarding this topic with the title *Rifqan Ahl as-Sunnah bi Ahl as-Sunnah*.[8] In its introduction I said [that],

> [t]here is no doubt that the obligation upon the People of the Sunnah in every time and place is mutual affection, compassion in what is between them, and cooperation upon reverence[9] and godliness.[10]
>
> Surely from what one regrets in this time is what occurred of alienation and differing from some of the People of the Sunnah; from what was caused by some of them being occupied with disparaging, cautioning [against], and boycotting others. The obligation was that their efforts be

---

[7] **[t]** I.e., their brothers.

[8] **[t]** I.e., *Gentleness, [O] People of the Sunnah, with the People of the Sunnah.*

[9] **[t]** Ar. birr (بِرّ) – reverence, piety; righteousness, probity; godliness, devoutness; kindness.

[10] **[t]** Ar. taqwâ (تَقْوَى) – godliness, devoutness, piety, reverence.

> collectively directed at others from the disbelievers and the People of Heresies hostile to the People of the Sunnah; that they be mutually affectionate and compassionate with regards to what is between them, mentioning one another with gentleness and lenience.

After the publication of this treatise, individuals from the People of the Sunnah objected to it—may Allah pardon us and them—and I pointed that out in what I wrote at the end of the treatise *al-Ḥathth 'alâ Ittibâ' as-Sunnah wat-Taḥdhîr min al-Bida' wa Bayân Khaṭarihâ.*[11] At the forefront of these [individuals] who objected to this treatise were those from whom I sought gentleness with their brothers from the People of the Sunnah. By "the People of the Sunnah" in [the title] *Rifqan Ahl as-Sunnah bi Ahl as-Sunnah* I did not mean the sects and parties deviating from what the People of the Sunnah are upon; such as those whose party arose from al-Manṣūrah in Egypt;[12] such as the squatters in London

---

[11] **[t]** I.e., *Urging Adherence to the Sunnah, Cautioning from the Heresies, and the Clarification of Their Significance.* See the last two chapters of this translation.

[12] **[t]** This footnote, along with footnotes nos. 12i, 12ii, 13, and 14 were originally part of the main text of the treatise. I have made them into footnotes to help the text's flow and readability in English. **[a]** Addressing his followers, this party's founder said, "Thus your call is more deserving of [having] the people come to it and it not coming to anyone ... since it is comprised of every good, while others are not free from deficiency."[i] He also said,

> Our position on the various calls which prevailed in this era, divided the hearts and troubled the thoughts is that we weigh them by the scale of our call. Thus, whatever agrees with it, then welcome! And whatever differs with it, then we are free of it. We believe that our call is universal and does not leave a righteous part of any call except that it touches on it briefly and points it out!!![ii]

This speech necessitates that they welcome the Râfiḍî if he agrees with them and that they free themselves from those who differ with them, even if they were Sunnîs upon the way of the Predecessors. **[t]** Here the shaikh is speaking of the Muslim Brotherhood (Ar. al-ikhwân al-muslimūn (الإخوان المسلمون) – lit. the Muslim brothers).

who wage war against the People of the Sunnah by what they spread in their magazine, which they have called *as-Sunnah*;[13] and such as those whose call arose from Delhi in India.[14]

I surely emphasized the counsel to the youth of the People of the Sunnah in this introduction to be concerned with being occupied with knowledge; to occupy their times with its acquisition in order that they seize profit and be safe from the cheating that was mentioned in the Messenger's ﷺ statement, «Two blessings which many of the people are cheated of: health and spare time.»[15] From the most important books of the contemporary scholars that they should be concerned with reading are: *Majmū' al-Fatâwâ* of our shaikh, the imam[16] of the People of the Sunnah during his time, Shaikh 'Abdul-'Azîz bin 'Abdillah bin Bâz ﷺ; the *Fatâwâ* of the [Saudi Arabian] Permanent Committee for Academic Researches and Verdicts; the writings of our shaikh, the 'allâmah, Shaikh Muḥammad al-

---

[12i] al-Bannâ, Shaikh Ḥasan. *Mudhakkirât ad-Da'wah wad-Dâ'iyyah*. Dâr ash-Shihâb. pg. 232.
[12ii] al-Bannâ, Shaikh Ḥasan. *Majmū'ah Risâ'il Ḥasan al-Bannâ*. Dâr ad-Da'wah, 1411H. pg. 240.
[13] From that is their derogation of the scholars of the Kingdom of Saudi Arabia and their describing the callers who are like them in it as liberals due to their display of opposition and derogation of the scholars, especially the [ones in] authority amongst them!! And one of the distinguished [scholars] has written a treatise titled, *Mujallah as-Sunnah???*, in which he gathered a sum of that from their magazine. **[t]** Here the shaikh is speaking of Muḥammad Surūr Zain al-'Âbidîn and his followers (a.k.a., the Surūrîs).
[14] [This call] does not deviate from six points and ignorance and lack of comprehension in the religion prevail over its people. In their call, they do not turn to the most important of the important matters, i.e., singling Allah out in worship and keeping away from polytheism, i.e., the call of the Messengers, collectively, as Allah, exalted is He, said, **(And We had certainly dispatched in every nation a Messenger [preaching] that you worship Allah and avoid the false gods) (16:36)**. So indeed, those tested by supplicating to the companions of the graves, appealing for aid through them, and slaughtering for them, they (i.e., the Messengers) have no share in their call! **[t]** Here the shaikh is speaking of Tablighi Jamaat (Ar. jamâ'ah at-tablîgh (جَماعة التبليغ) – lit. the group of conveying).
[15] It was published by al-Bukhârî in his *Ṣaḥîḥ* (no. 6412) and is the first ḥadîth in *Kitâb ar-Riqâq*.
[16] **[t]** Ar. imâm (إمام) – leader, head. It is the honorific given to the head or heads of a particular group, whether it be a top scholar of the religion or the ruler of the Muslims.

Amîn ash-Shinqîṭî ﷺ—especially *Aḍwâ' al-Bayân fî Îḍâḥ al-Qur'ân bil-Qur'ân*; and the writings of the two formidable scholars, Shaikh Muḥammad bin Ṣâliḥ al-'Uthaimîn and Shaikh Muḥammad Nâṣir ad-Dîn al-Albânî ﷺ.

I also advise the students of knowledge in every land to benefit from those occupied with knowledge from the People of the Sunnah in that land; like Shaikh al-Albânî's pupils in Jordan who established a centre after him in his name,[17] like Shaikh Muḥammad al-Maghrâwî in Morocco, Shaikh Muḥammad 'Alî Farkūs and Shaikh al-'Îd Sharîfî in Algeria, and others from the People of the Sunnah. From the advice to the People of the Sunnah is that whoever of them erred should be notified of his error, not pursued for it. Innocence from him should not be declared because of that and benefit should be sought from him, especially if no one is found who is more prominent in knowledge and virtue than he.

I advise the youth to be cautioned against being occupied with following the stumblings of the students of knowledge and following the internet sites concerned with gathering their slips and cautioning against them because of [these slips]. Shaikh Muḥammad bin Sulaimân al-Ashqar had erred slanderously in the derogation of the companion Abî Bakrah ﷺ and his narrations, and [in] his[18] concern with the issue of the woman's guardianship and in her sharing in the appointment [as guardian] of others. I refuted him in a treatise titled, *ad-Difâ' 'an aṣ-Ṣaḥâbî Abî Bakrah wa Marwiyâtih wal-Istidlâl li Man' Wilâyah an-Nisâ' 'alâr-Rijâl,*[19] and when I cautioned against his repugnant slip

---

[17] **[t]** I.e., Shaikhs 'Alî Ḥasan al-Ḥalabî, Salîm bin 'Îd al-Hilâlî, Muḥammad Mūsâ Naṣr, Mash·hūr Ḥasan Salmân, Ḥusain bin 'Awdah al-'Awâyishah, and others.

[18] **[t]** I.e., Shaikh Muḥammad bin Sulaimân al-Ashqar's.

[19] **[t]** I.e., *Defending the Companion Abî Bakrah and His Narrations, and Evidence for the Prevention of the Women's Guardianship Over Men.*

I did not caution against his beneficial writings; among the men of the two *Ṣaḥîḥs*, as well as other [books], are narrators described with heresy whose narrations were accepted despite the People of Knowledge's notification of those heresies in order to caution against them.

In the beginning of Ramaḍân of 1423H, six months before the publication of *Rifqan Ahl as-Sunnah bi Ahl as-Sunnah*, I forwarded a letter of advice to one of those who the youth of the People of the Sunnah were affected by.[20] He had replied with a polite letter in which he supplicated to Allah to benefit him with this advice and mentioned that he advised the one who I referred to in the letter.[21] I ask Allah ﷻ to grant him and me, as well as the rest of our brothers from the People of the Sunnah, success for all of what returns with good and the praiseworthy outcome; and that He keeps everybody away from all of what returns with harms and the disastrous outcome, in the worldly [life] and [in] the Afterlife. Surely, He is hearing [and] respondent. What follows is what has come in this letter [of mine]:

And so I surely write these words to your eminence in hopes that you accept them with an eye of consideration, while «the religion is [sincere] advice» and «the believer to the believer is like the building; they strengthen one another.» From the right of the Muslim upon the Muslim is his advice and cooperation with him upon the good.

1. During the meeting with your eminence which recently came to an end, you mentioned to me that you were greater than I in age; in these days I had entered into the eightieth

---

[20] **[t]** I.e., Shaikh Rabî' bin Hâdî al-Madkhalî.

[21] **[t]** I.e., Shaikh Fâliḥ bin Nâfi' al-Ḥarbî.

decade[22] and according to this, you had preceded in this decade. Accordingly then, surely my being from those who taught you in 1381H and what was after it is from the seniors' narrating from the minors.[23] The likes of you and I are in need of being distracted from all of what results in disunity between the People of the Sunnah by beneficial knowledge.

2. Some time ago, I had previously heard a word from you: that you were distracted from being occupied with the Qur'an and pondering on its meanings by being busy with Ḥadîth and its men.[24] I say you are now distracted from the Qur'an and Ḥadîth by speaking about some of the People of the Sunnah, and others. From what has distracted you from being occupied with the knowledge of the Book and the Sunnah is battling with those who are not from the People of the Sunnah and [with] those who the traces of tribulations, the belittling of the scholars' status with the claim of their lack of comprehending current [events], have occurred from—[which] without doubt, is in its place. That which is not in its place, however, is the tendency for following up the errors of those who are from the People of the Sunnah and defaming them due to their not agreeing with you in some opinions; frequently being occupied with the likes of these is unbefitting. If the mention of some of their errors occurs, then being preoccupied with them, reiterating them,

---

[22] **[t]** I.e., his 70s. Being about a year or so older than Shaikh 'Abdul-Muḥsin, Shaikh Rabî' bin Hâdî was one of the shaikh's students while studying at the Islamic University of Madînah. Shaikh Rabî' mentioned this fact publicly during the height of the turmoil described above by Shaikh 'Abdul-Muḥsin, and was subsequently translated and posted on some English internet message boards.

[23] **[t]** Ar. riwâyah al-akâbir 'an al-aṣâghir (رواية الأكابر عن الأصاغر) – lit. the seniors' narration from the minors. **[a]** Just as [is mentioned] in *Nuzhah an-Naḍhr Sharḥ Nukhbah al-Fikr* by Ḥâfiḍh Ibn Ḥajar, the seniors' narrating from the minors is the narrator's narrating from those who are below him age, meeting i.e., meeting the shaikhs, or in degree.

[24] **[t]** I.e., its narrators.

and making them the talk of sittings is unbefitting. Then with discussing them, you get angry and raise your voice—and surely that, with respect to what contains danger, has an affect on your health.

3. Mention of disparagement and accreditation, as well as talk about some of the People of the Sunnah and others has become common in these days. The spreading of that on the internet is from what caused the questions to [successively] arrive from Europe, America, North Africa, and other [countries], about some of those whose disparagement occurred from you and Shaikh...[25] along with Shaikh's[26] expanding the talk to the honours of the shaikhs and students of knowledge—domestic and foreign—whose lectures and writings Allah caused benefit with, to cautioning against them, and what results from that of deserting [one another] and mutual aversion; the Messenger r said, «Be welcoming, do not be alienating. And be easy, do not be difficult.» His encouragement to good should be desired for the mistaken person from the People of the Sunnah, along with notifying him of his error, if his error is clear. He should not be opposed, nor abandoned, nor should seeking benefit from him be cautioned against.

Although I believe that you do not agree with him regarding some of his speech about individuals, because of the association which is between you and Shaikh ...[27] and the connection of disparagement to you and him, what is not from you could be thought to be attributed to you. Due to this, the hope for you is that you do not occupy yourself with the disparaging of those who are from the People of the Sunnah, and that you have a

---

[25] **[t]** See footnote no. 21.
[26] **[t]** Ibid.
[27] **[t]** Ibid.

position with regards to him that is restricted to its limit such that the students of knowledge and others, domestic and foreign, are safe from being occupied with 'it was said' and 'he said'[28] and the successive questions: What is your statement regarding the disparagement of so-and-so, or so-and-so by so-and-so, or so-and-so (although there is no connection between you and this person)? You are well known for diligence in learning and teaching, and you have beneficial writings. You surpassed your colleagues in the days of study and you have useful writings regarding knowledge. As for him,[29] then he was from the last of his colleagues and his grading at passing [the exam] was 'good'.[30] He does not have seniority in knowledge, he does not have writings, and the bulk of his merchandise is being occupied with the honours of people; you have an example in the companions of Allah's Messenger r where after those who regretted what emanated from them, some of them said, "O people, question opinion in the religion!"

I ask Allah ﷻ to make us all successful in what He is pleased with, [to] show us the truth as truth and make us successful in adhering to it, and [to] show us falsehood as falsehood and make us successful in avoiding it; surely He is hearing [and] respondent.

The praise is Allah's, Lord of the worlds; and may Allah send salutations, peace, and blessings upon His servant and Messenger, our Prophet Muḥammad, upon his family and his companions.

---

[28] **[t]** Ar. al-qîl wal-qâl (القِيل والقال) – lit. the 'it was said' and the 'he said', referring to idle talk, gossip.

[29] **[t]** See footnote no. 21.

[30] **[t]** Ar. jayyid (جَيِّد) – good, perfect; outstanding, excellent; good (as in an examination grade, as opposed to mumtâz (مُمتاز) – passing with distinction).

بسم الله الرحمن الرحيم

Introduction to the First Edition[31]

The praise is for Allah, the One who united the hearts of the believers, desired union and harmony for them, and cautioned them against division and differing. I testify that there is no god [worthy of worship] except Allah alone; He has no partner. He created, then measured; He legislated, then facilitated; and He was compassionate with the believers. I testify that Muḥammad is His servant and Messenger who was commissioned with facilitating and the announcing of glad tidings, for he said, «Be easy, do not be difficult. And be welcoming, do not be alienating.»

O Allah, send salutations, peace, and blessings upon him, upon his purified family, his companions—those who He described as being harsh against the disbelievers and merciful between themselves—and upon whoever followed them in excellence until the Day of Reward. O Allah, guide me, guide for me, and guide by me. O Allah, purify my soul from rancour and

---

[31] **[t]** See footnote no. 3.

direct my tongue to speak the truth. O Allah, surely, I seek refuge with You lest I stray or be led astray, err or be caused to err, oppress or be oppressed, behave ignorantly or be treated ignorantly.

As for what follows, then the People of the Sunnah and Congregation are those who follow what Allah's Messenger ﷺ and his companions were upon. Their ascription is to the Messenger's ﷺ sunnah, which he urged adherence to with his statement, «So upon you is my sunnah and the sunnah of the Guided Successors after me. Adhere to it and bite onto it with the molar teeth.» He cautioned against opposing it with his statement, «Beware of the innovated affairs [in religion], for surely, every innovation is heresy, and every heresy is misguidance,» and his statement, «Whoever detested my sunnah, then he is not from me.» This is contrary to others from the People of Desires and Heresies who follow paths the Messenger ﷺ and his companions were not upon. The People of the Sunnah's creed manifested with the appearance of his ﷺ mission, while the creeds of the People of Desires were born after his ﷺ time. From them is what existed during the end of the Companions' lifetime and from them is what existed after that.

The Messenger ﷺ informed that whoever lived from his companions would see this division and differing, for he said, «Indeed, he who lives from you will see much differing.» He then guided to the path of the Straight Way, i.e., following his sunnah and the sunnah of his guided successors. He cautioned against the innovated affairs and informed that they are misguidance. It is not intelligible, nor is it acceptable, that he hid truth and guidance from the Companions ﷺ, saving it for the people to come after them. So surely, all of those innovated heresies are evil. If there were good in any of them, then the Companions certainly would have arrived at it [before others]. They are, however, an evil many of those who came after them—of those who deviated from what the Companions ﷺ were upon—have been tested by. Imam Mâlik ﷺ had said, "The last of this nation will not be corrected except by what corrected its first." Due to that, the People of the Sunnah are ascribed to the Sunnah, while others are ascribed to their false ascriptions, like the Jabarîs, the Qadarîs, the Murji'ah and the Twelver Imamîs;[32] or to the names of certain individuals like the Jahmîs, the Zaidîs, the Ash'arîs, and the Ibâḍîs—and it is not said in this respect that "the Wahhâbîs" is an ascription to Shaikh Muḥammad bin 'Abdil-Wahhâb ﷺ, because the People of the Sunnah during the time of Shaikh Muḥammad ﷺ never came with anything new such as to ascribe it to him. Rather, he was an adherent to what the Righteous Predecessors were upon, an endorser of the Sunnah, a propagator of it, and a caller to it. Those full of hatred, however, apply this ascription to Shaikh Muḥammad bin 'Abdil-Wahhâb's ﷺ reformist call to confuse the people. [In doing so], they turned them[33] away from following the truth and guidance, and they caused them to remain upon what they were upon of innovated heresies [that are in] opposition to what the People of the Sunnah and Congregation were upon.

In *al-I'tisâm* (1/79), Imam ash-Shâṭibî said,

> 'Abdur-Raḥman bin Mahdî said, "Imam Mâlik had been asked about the Sunnah and he said, 'It is what has no name other than the Sunnah,' then he recited,

---

[32] **[t]** I.e., the Râfiḍî Shî'ah.

[33] **[t]** I.e., the people.

﴿ وَأَنَّ هَٰذَا صِرَٰطِي مُسْتَقِيمًا فَٱتَّبِعُوهُ ۖ وَلَا تَتَّبِعُوا۟ ٱلسُّبُلَ فَتَفَرَّقَ بِكُمْ عَن سَبِيلِهِۦ ۚ ﴾

(And that this is my straight way, so follow it and do not follow [other] paths, for they will separate you from His way) (6:153).

In *Madârij as-Sâlikîn* (3/179), Ibn al-Qayyim said, "Some of the imams had been asked about the Sunnah and they said, '[It is] what has no name other than the Sunnah,' meaning that the People of the Sunnah do not have another name they are ascribed to."

And in *Kitâb al-Intifâ'* by Ibn 'Abdil-Barr (pg. 35), [it is mentioned] "that a man asked [Imam] Mâlik, 'Who are the People of the Sunnah?' He said, 'The People of the Sunnah are those who do not have a title they are known by; not Jahmî, not Qadarî, not Râfiḍî.'"

There is no doubt that the obligation upon the People of the Sunnah in every time and place is mutual affection, compassion in what is between them, and cooperation upon reverence and godliness.

Surely from what one regrets in this time is what occurred of alienation and differing from some of the People of the Sunnah; from what was caused by some of them being occupied with disparaging, cautioning [against], and boycotting others. The obligation was that their efforts be collectively directed at others from the disbelievers and the People of Heresies hostile to the People of the Sunnah; that they be mutually affectionate and compassionate with regards to what is between them, mentioning one another with gentleness and lenience.

I had considered writing words as an advice to all of these [people], asking Allah ﷻ that He causes benefit with these words. Surely, I only want rectification of what I am able and my success is not possible except by Allah; upon Him I rely and to Him I repent. I have named this advice, *Gentleness,* [O] *People of the Sunnah, with the People of the Sunnah.*

I ask Allah for the success and the correctness for all, that He rectifies their discord, unifies their hearts, guides them to the paths of peace, and brings them from the darknesses into the light; surely, He is hearing and respondent.

The Grace of [Articulated] Speech and Clarification

Allah's graces upon His slaves cannot be counted, nor enumerated. From the greatest of these graces is the [articulated] speech with which the person clarifies his intent, says the straight word, and commands the recognized [good acts] and prohibits the reprehensible [acts]. Whoever is deprived of it, these affairs do not arise for him. Mutual understanding with others is not possible for him except by gesturing or writing—if he could write. Allah ﷻ said,

﴿ وَضَرَبَ ٱللَّهُ مَثَلًا رَّجُلَيۡنِ أَحَدُهُمَآ أَبۡكَمُ لَا يَقۡدِرُ
عَلَىٰ شَيۡءٖ وَهُوَ كَلٌّ عَلَىٰ مَوۡلَىٰهُ أَيۡنَمَا يُوَجِّههُّ لَا يَأۡتِ
بِخَيۡرٍ هَلۡ يَسۡتَوِي هُوَ وَمَن يَأۡمُرُ بِٱلۡعَدۡلِ وَهُوَ عَلَىٰ صِرَٰطٖ
مُّسۡتَقِيمٖ ﴾

(And Allah puts forward an example of two men. One of them is dumb, not having power over anything and he is a burden to his master. Whichever way he directs him he brings no

good. Is such a man equal to one who commands justice and is himself on a Straight Way?) (16:76).

In its exegesis, it has been said, "Surely, it is an example put forth by Allah of Himself and of the idol." It was said, "Surely, it is an example of the disbeliever and the believer." al-Qurṭubî said (9/149), "It was narrated from Ibn 'Abbâs ﷺ and it is acceptable, because it[34] is general," and it is clear in the deficiency of the dumb slave who does not benefit others and whose master does not benefit from him, whichever way he directs him.

Allah ﷻ said,

﴿ فَوَرَبِّ ٱلسَّمَآءِ وَٱلۡأَرۡضِ إِنَّهُۥ لَحَقٌّ مِّثۡلَ مَآ أَنَّكُمۡ تَنطِقُونَ ﴾

(Then, by the Lord of the heaven and the earth, indeed it is certainly truth, similar to [the fact] that you can speak) (51:23).

Surely, Allah has sworn by Himself on the certainty of the resurrection and the reward for deeds, just as the [articulated] speech is currently occurring for those addressed; and in that is an allusion to the grace of [articulated] speech.

He, glorified is He, said,

﴿ خَلَقَ ٱلۡإِنسَٰنَ ۝ عَلَّمَهُ ٱلۡبَيَانَ ﴾

(He created man! He taught him the clarification) (55:3-4).

---

[34] **[t]** I.e., the verse.

Al-Ḥasan explained 'the clarification' as [articulated] speech; and in that is an allusion to the grace of [articulated] speech by which the person's explanation arises from what he intends.

He, exalted is He, said,

﴿ أَلَمْ نَجْعَل لَّهُۥ عَيْنَيْنِ ۝ وَلِسَانًا وَشَفَتَيْنِ ﴾

(Have We not made for him a pair of eyes! a tongue and two lips?) (90:8-9).

In his *Tafsîr*, Ibn Kathîr said,

> His statement, exalted is He, (Have We not made for him a pair of eyes,) meaning he sees with them; (a tongue,) meaning he speaks with it, and thus expresses what is inside him; (and two lips,) he seeks aid from them for speech, eating food, and beautification for his face and mouth.

From the known [facts] is that certainly this grace truly becomes a grace when the [articulated] speech is used for what is good. As for when it is used for evil, then it is a curse upon its companion and whoever was deprived of this grace is better off than him.

Preserving the Tongue from Speech Except in Good

Allah عز وجل said,

﴿ يَـٰٓأَيُّهَا ٱلَّذِينَ ءَامَنُوا۟ ٱتَّقُوا۟ ٱللَّهَ وَقُولُوا۟ قَوْلًا سَدِيدًا ¤
يُصْلِحْ لَكُمْ أَعْمَـٰلَكُمْ وَيَغْفِرْ لَكُمْ ذُنُوبَكُمْ ۗ وَمَن يُطِعِ ٱللَّهَ
وَرَسُولَهُۥ فَقَدْ فَازَ فَوْزًا عَظِيمًا ﴾

(O you who believed, be godly to Allah and say a right word! He will rectify your deeds for you and forgive your sins for you; and whoever obeys Allah and His Messenger, then surely he has achieved a tremendous success) (33:70-71).

He عز وجل said,

﴿ يَـٰٓأَيُّهَا ٱلَّذِينَ ءَامَنُوا۟ ٱجْتَنِبُوا۟ كَثِيرًا مِّنَ ٱلظَّنِّ إِنَّ بَعْضَ
ٱلظَّنِّ إِثْمٌ ۖ وَلَا تَجَسَّسُوا۟ وَلَا يَغْتَب بَّعْضُكُم بَعْضًا ۚ أَيُحِبُّ

أَحَدُكُمْ أَن يَأْكُلَ لَحْمَ أَخِيهِ مَيْتًا فَكَرِهْتُمُوهُ ۚ

وَٱتَّقُوا۟ ٱللَّهَ ۚ إِنَّ ٱللَّهَ تَوَّابٌ رَّحِيمٌ ﴾

(O you who believed, avoid much of the assumption! Surely, part of the assumption is sin. And do not spy, nor backbite one another. Would one of you want to eat the flesh of his dead brother? Surely you would hate it. And be godly to Allah; surely Allah is an acceptor [of repentance, and] compassionate) (49:12).

He, exalted is He, said,

﴿ وَلَقَدْ خَلَقْنَا ٱلْإِنسَـٰنَ وَنَعْلَمُ مَا تُوَسْوِسُ بِهِۦ نَفْسُهُۥ ۖ

وَنَحْنُ أَقْرَبُ إِلَيْهِ مِنْ حَبْلِ ٱلْوَرِيدِ ۝ إِذْ يَتَلَقَّى ٱلْمُتَلَقِّيَانِ

عَنِ ٱلْيَمِينِ وَعَنِ ٱلشِّمَالِ قَعِيدٌ ۝ مَّا يَلْفِظُ مِن قَوْلٍ إِلَّا

لَدَيْهِ رَقِيبٌ عَتِيدٌ ﴾

(We have indeed created man and We know what his own soul whispers to him. We are closer to him than his jugular vein, ! since the two receivers [who] receive from the right and from the left are supervisors. He does not utter a statement except that he has a watcher prepared [to record it]) (50:16-18).

He, exalted is He, said,

﴿ وَٱلَّذِينَ يُؤْذُونَ ٱلْمُؤْمِنِينَ وَٱلْمُؤْمِنَٰتِ بِغَيْرِ مَا
ٱكْتَسَبُوا۟ فَقَدِ ٱحْتَمَلُوا۟ بُهْتَٰنًا وَإِثْمًا مُّبِينًا ﴾

(And those who annoy believing men and women for other than what they earned, indeed bear [the burden of] slander and manifest sin) (33:58).

In *Ṣaḥîḥ Muslim* (no. 2589) from Abî Hurairah رضي الله عنه, [it is recorded] that,

> Allah's Messenger ﷺ [asked], «Do you know what backbiting is?» They said, "Allah and His Messenger are more knowledgeable." He said, «[It is] your mentioning of your brother with what he detests.» It was [asked], "So then do you see [it as backbiting] if my brother has what I said?" He said, «If he had what you said, then you have backbitten him. If he did not have it, then you have slandered him.»

Allah عز وجل said,

﴿ وَلَا تَقْفُ مَا لَيْسَ لَكَ بِهِۦ عِلْمٌ ۚ إِنَّ ٱلسَّمْعَ وَٱلْبَصَرَ
وَٱلْفُؤَادَ كُلُّ أُو۟لَٰٓئِكَ كَانَ عَنْهُ مَسْـُٔولًا ﴾

(Do not follow what you do not have knowledge of. Surely, the hearing, the sight, and the heart, will all be questioned about it) (17:36).

From Abî Hurairah ⁂, [who] said, Allah's Messenger ⁂ said,
> «Surely Allah is pleased with three [things] for you
> and He detests three [things] for you. He is pleased
> for you that you worship Him, that you do not
> associate anything with Him, and that you all
> adhere to Allah's rope and not be divided. He
> detests for you 'it was said' and 'it is said',
> excessive questioning, and the wasting of
> wealth.»[35]

From Abî Hurairah ⁂, from the Prophet ⁂, [who] said,
> «The son of Adam's share of fornication was
> written for him, attaining that unavoidably.
> Indeed, the eyes' fornication is the sight; the ears'
> fornication is the hearing; the tongue's fornication
> is the speech; the hand's fornication is the touch;
> the foot's fornication is the step; and the heart
> wishes and desires, the private parts testify to that
> and deny it.»[36]

In his *Ṣaḥîḥ* (no. 10), al-Bukhârî narrated from 'Abdillah bin 'Amr ⁂, from the Prophet ⁂ [who] said,
> «The Muslim is whose tongue and hands the
> [other] Muslims are safe from.»[37]

---

[35] Published by Muslim (no. 1715); these three detested things came in the ḥadîth of al-Mughîrah with al-Bukhârî (no. 2408) and Muslim.

[36] Narrated by al-Bukhârî (no. 6612) and Muslim (no. 2657); the wording is Muslim's.

[37] Muslim narrated it in his *Ṣaḥîḥ* and its wording was: "that a man asked Allah's Messenger ⁂, 'Which of the Muslims is best?' He said, «Whoever's tongue and hands the [other] Muslims are safe from.» Muslim also narrated from the ḥadîth of Jâbir (no. 65) with the wording of the ḥadîth of 'Abdillah bin 'Amr with al-Bukhârî.

In the ḥadîth's explanation, Ḥâfiḍh[38] [Ibn Ḥajar al-'Asqalânî] said,

> The ḥadîth is general with regards to the tongue with the exception of the hands, because [with] the tongue, speech is possible regarding those who have passed, those who are present and those who come after, unlike the hand. Yes! It is possible that the tongue shares in that by writing. And indeed, its affects in that are great.

In this regard, the poet says,

> I wrote and have ascertained the day of my writing,
> because my hand will perish and its writing will remain.
> So if I did good, it will be rewarded with its like.
> And if I did evil, then upon me is its reckoning.

In his *Ṣaḥîḥ* (no. 6474), al-Bukhârî narrated from Sahl bin Sa'd ﷺ from Allah's Messenger ﷺ [who] said,

> «Whoever safeguards what is between his jaws and what is between his legs for me, I safeguard Paradise for him.»

The intent of what is between the jaws and legs is the tongue and the private parts, [respectively].

[38] **[t]** Ar. ḥâfiḍh (حافظ) – memorizer, preserver. It is the honorific given to a traditionist with exceptional skills in memorising Prophetic traditions. It also refers to a memorizer of the Qur'an.

In [their] Ṣaḥīḥs, al-Bukhârî (no. 6475) and Muslim (no. 74) [narrated] from Abî Hurairah ☀ from Allah's Messenger ﷺ [who] said,

«Whoever believes in Allah and the Last Day, then let him speak good or be silent,» [to the end of] the ḥadîth.

In *Sharḥ al-Arba'în*, regarding this ḥadîth's explanation, an-Nawawî said,

Ash-Shâfi'î said, "The ḥadîth's meaning is when one wants to speak, then let him ponder. So, if it became apparent that there is no harm upon him, he can speak. And if it became apparent that it contains harm and doubt, he should hold back." And it was conveyed by some of them that he said, "If you were to buy the paper for the ḥafaḍhah,[39] indeed you would remain silent over much of the speech."

On pg. 45 of his book, *Rawḍah al-'Uqalâ' wa Nuzhah al-Fuḍalâ'*, Imam Abū Ḥâtim bin Ḥibbân al-Bustî said,

The obligation upon the sensible [person] is that he maintains silence until speaking is necessary for him. For how many more are those who regretted when they spoke and [how] fewer are those who regret when they remained silent. The longest of the people in misery and the greatest of them in being tested are those who have been

---

[39] **[t]** Ar. ḥafaḍhah (حَفَظَة) – the angels who record the people's deeds. See *Mukhtâr as-Ṣiḥâḥ*.

> tested by an unrestrained tongue and a closed heart.

On pg. 47, he also said,

> The sensible [person's] tongue is behind his heart. So when he intends the statement, he returns to the heart. If it was for him, he spoke, and if not, then no. The ignorant person, his heart is on the tip of his tongue; whatever comes upon his tongue he speaks with. Whoever does not preserve his tongue does not make sense of his religion.

In [their] *Ṣaḥîḥs*, al-Bukhârî (no. 6477) and Muslim (no. 2988) narrated from Abî Hurairah ﷺ that Allah's Messenger ﷺ said,

> «Surely, the servant will certainly speak a word not noticing what it contains. Due to it, he will be thrown into the Fire farther than what is between the east and the west.»[40]

At the end of the ḥadîth of the Prophet's ﷺ counsel to Mu'âdh,[41] in reply to Mu'âdh's ﷺ [question], "O Prophet of Allah, will we be held accountable for what we speak with?" he ﷺ said,

> «Are people thrown down into the Hellfire upon their faces—or upon their noses—except [by] the harvests of their tongues?»

In his explanation from his book, *al-Jâmi' al-'Ulūm wal-Ḥikam* (2/147), Ḥâfidh Ibn Rajab said,

---

[40] The wording is Muslim's.

[41] Published by at-Tirmidhî (no. 2616), and [concerning the ḥadîth], he said, "An authentic good ḥadîth."

> The intent of 'the harvests of the tongues' is the forbidden speech's reward and punishment, because the person plants the good deeds and the misdeeds with his statement and his deed. On the Day of Standing, he then harvests what he planted. So whoever planted good from a statement or a deed, he will harvest the honour, while whoever planted evil from a statement or a deed, he will harvest the tomorrow of remorse... "This indicates that restraining the tongue, seizing it and confining it is the basis of all the good and that whoever controlled his tongue has controlled his affair, fortified it and seized it."[42]

He conveyed from Yūnus bin 'Ubaid that he said, "I have not seen from anyone whose tongue was on a mind,[43] except [that] I saw that[44] as goodness in the rest of his deeds," and from Yaḥyâ bin Abî Kathîr that he said, "The speech of a person is not proper unless you recognize that in the rest of his deeds, while the speech of a person is not corrupted at all unless you recognize that in the rest of his deeds."[45]

In his *Ṣaḥîḥ* (no. 2581), Muslim narrated from Abî Hurairah that Allah's Messenger ﷺ [asked],

> «Do you know who the bankrupt [person] is?» They said, "According to us, the bankrupt [person] is whoever does not have a dirham, nor any property." So he said, «Surely, the bankrupt

---

[42] *al-Jâmi' al-'Ulūm wal-Ḥikam*, (2/146).
[43] **[t]** I.e., he was mindful of what he says.
[44] **[t]** I.e., his mindfulness.
[45] *al-Jâmi' al-'Ulūm wal-Ḥikam*, (1/149).

[person] from my nation comes on the Day of
Standing with prayer, fasting and zakâh, while he
comes having abused this [person], slandered this
[person], having eaten the wealth of this [person],
having shed the blood of this [person], and having
beaten this [person]. So this [person] will be given
from his good deeds and this [person] from his
good deeds. Then if his good deeds are spent
before he settles what is upon him, it is taken from
their sins. So they are flung upon him, then he is
thrown into the Fire.»

In his Ṣaḥîḥ (no. 2564), Muslim narrated a long ḥadîth from Abî
Hurairah ⁕. At its end came,

«It is enough evil for a person that he despises
his Muslim brother. Everything of the Muslim is
sacred to the Muslim: his blood, his wealth and
his honour.»

In their Ṣaḥîḥs, al-Bukhârî (no. 1739) and Muslim narrated from
Ibn 'Abbâs ⁕,

that Allah's Messenger ﷺ addressed the people on
the Day of Slaughter[46] and [asked], «O people,
which day is this?» They said, "A sacred day." He
[asked], «Which city is this?» They said, "A sacred
city." He [asked], «Then which month is this?»
They said, "A sacred month." He said, «Then surely
your blood, your wealth, and your honours are
sacred to you just like the sacredness of this day of

---

[46] **[t]** I.e., the 10th of Dhil-Ḥijjah, the first day of 'Îd al-Aḍḥâ.

yours, in this city of yours, in this month of yours.» Then he repeated it several times, raised his head and [asked], «O Allah, have I conveyed?» Ibn 'Abbâs ﴿ said, "For, by the One whose hand my soul is in, indeed, it was certainly his counsel to his nation. 'So let the witness convey to the absent. Do not return as disbelievers after me, some of you striking the necks of others.'[47]

In his *Ṣaḥîḥ* (no. 2674), Muslim narrated from Abî Hurairah ﴿ that Allah's Messenger ﷺ said,

«Whoever called to guidance will have the likes of the rewards of whoever followed him and that would not diminish anything from their rewards. And whoever called to misguidance will have upon him the likes of the offences of whoever followed him and that would not diminish anything from their offences.»

In *at-Targhîb wat-Tarhîb* (1/65), commenting on the ḥadîth, «When the son of Adam dies, his deeds cease except from one of three ... ,» [to the end of] the ḥadîth, Ḥâfidḥ al-Mundhirî said,

The transcriber of beneficial knowledge has his reward and the reward of whoever read it, copied it, or acted upon it after him, as long as his writing and the acting upon it remains, because of this ḥadîth and its likes. The transcriber of [what is] non-beneficial from what obligates offence, upon him is his burden and the burden of whoever read

---

[47] The wording is al-Bukhârî's.

> it, copied it, or acted upon it after him, as long as his writing and the acting upon it remains, because of what has preceded from the ḥâdîths, «whoever established a good or evil sunnah.» And Allah is more knowledgeable.

In his *Ṣaḥîḥ* (no. 6502), al-Bukhârî narrated from Abî Hurairah ﷺ [who] said, "Allah's Messenger ﷺ said,

> «Surely Allah said, "Whoever makes an ally of Mine an enemy, then I will surely declare war on him,"» [to the end of] the ḥadîth.

ASSUMPTION AND SPYING

The Most High said,

﴿ يَـٰٓأَيُّهَا ٱلَّذِينَ ءَامَنُوا۟ ٱجْتَنِبُوا۟ كَثِيرًا مِّنَ ٱلظَّنِّ إِنَّ بَعْضَ ٱلظَّنِّ إِثْمٌ ۖ وَلَا تَجَسَّسُوا۟ ﴾

(O you who believed, avoid much of the assumption! Surely, part of the assumption is sin. And do not spy) (49:12).

Surely this noble verse contains the command to avoid a lot of the assumption, that some of it is an offence, and the prohibition against spying. Spying is searching for the people's faults; and it is certainly what occurs in consequence of poor assumption. He ﷺ said,

> «Beware of assumption, for surely assumption is the most untruthful of speech. Do not probe [for each others faults]. Do not spy [on each other]. Do not be envious [of each other]. Do not have mutual hatred [towards each other]. Do not have disparity

[amongst each other]. Be Allah's servants, as brothers.»[48]

In his exegesis of a verse in chapter al-Ḥujurât (ch. 49), Ibn Kathîr mentioned [that] the Commander of the Believers, 'Umar bin al-Khaṭṭâb ☙ said, "Only assume good of a word that comes from your believing brother and find a good understanding for it."

As [mentioned] in his biography in *Tahdhîb at-Tahdhîb*, Bakr bin 'Abdillah al-Muzanî said, "Beware of the words in which if you were correct, you would not be rewarded, and if you erred in them, you would have offended, i.e., poor assumption of your brother."

And as mentioned in *al-Ḥilyah* (2/285) by Abî Nu'aim, Abū Qilâbah 'Abdullah bin Zaid al-Jazmî said, "If something you dislike was conveyed to you from your brother, then search your utmost for the excuse for him. Then if you do not find for him an excuse, say to yourself, 'I hope my brother has an excuse I do not know of'."

Sufyân bin Ḥusain said, "I mentioned a man in an ill [manner] near Iyâs bin Mu'âwiyah, so he looked at my face and [asked], 'Did you invade Rome?' I said, 'No.' He [asked], 'Then Sind, India, and the Turks?' I said, 'No.' He said, 'So Rome, Sind, India, and the Turks are safe from you, [but] your Muslim brother is not safe from you?!'" He said, "So I did not repeat it after it."[49]

I say how good is this reply from Iyâs ibn Mu'âwiyah who was famous for intelligence; and this reply is an example of his intelligence.

---

[48] Narrated by al-Bukhârî (no. 6064) and Muslim (no. 2563).
[49] *al-Bidâyah wan-Nihâyah* by Ibn Kathîr, (13/121).

In *Rawḍah al-'Uqalâ'* (pg. 131), Abū Ḥâtim bin Ḥibbân al-Bustî said,

> The obligation upon the sensible [person] is the need of well-being by the leaving of spying on the people's faults with being occupied with correcting his own faults. For surely, whoever is occupied with his own faults in place of others' faults relieves his body and does not tire his heart. So the more he examines his own fault, he attaches no importance to what he sees of its like from his brother. And surely, whoever is occupied with the people's faults in place of his own faults, his heart becomes blind, his body becomes tired and it becomes difficult for him to leave his own faults.

And on pg. 133, he said,

> Spying is from the branches of hypocrisy, just as good assumptions are from the branches of faith. The sensible [person] has good assumptions of his brothers and stands alone with his griefs and his sorrows, just as the ignorant [person] has poor assumptions of his brothers and is not reminded of his crimes and his anxieties.

Gentleness and Lenience

Allah described His Prophet Muḥammad ﷺ as being upon a tremendous character, for He said,

﴿ وَإِنَّكَ لَعَلَىٰ خُلُقٍ عَظِيمٍ ﴾

(And you are surely upon a tremendous character) (68:4).

He described him with gentleness and lenience, for He said,

﴿ فَبِمَا رَحْمَةٍ مِّنَ ٱللَّهِ لِنتَ لَهُمْ ۖ وَلَوْ كُنتَ فَظًّا غَلِيظَ ٱلْقَلْبِ لَٱنفَضُّوا۟ مِنْ حَوْلِكَ ۖ ﴾

(So because of mercy from Allah, you were lenient with them. If you were crude, harsh-hearted, they would have broken away from around you) (3:159).

He described him with mercy and graciousness with the believers, for He said,

﴿لَقَدْ جَآءَكُمْ رَسُولٌ مِّنْ أَنفُسِكُمْ عَزِيزٌ عَلَيْهِ مَا عَنِتُّمْ حَرِيصٌ عَلَيْكُم بِٱلْمُؤْمِنِينَ رَءُوفٌ رَّحِيمٌ﴾

(A Messenger has certainly come to you from yourselves. What distresses you is hurtful for him. [He is] eager for you; gracious [and] compassionate with the believers) (9:128).

The Messenger ﷺ commanded gentleness and desired it, for he said,

> «Be easy and do not be difficult; be welcoming and do not be alienating.»[50]

In his *Ṣaḥîḥ* (no. 220), al-Bukhârî narrated from Abî Hurairah رضي الله عنه that in the story of the Bedouin who urinated in the mosque, Allah's Messenger ﷺ said to his Companions,

> «Invite him and spill a bucket of water or a tumbler of water on his urine. For you were certainly sent as facilitators, you were not sent as those who make things difficult.»

Al-Bukhârî narrated (no. 6927) from 'Â'ishah رضي الله عنها that Allah's Messenger ﷺ said,

[50] Published by al-Bukhârî (no. 69) and Muslim (no. 1734) from the ḥadîth of Anas. Muslim published it from Abî Mūsâ and its wording is, «Be welcoming and do not be alienating; be easy and do not be difficult.»

> «O 'Â'ishah! surely Allah is gentle; He loves gentleness in all of the affair.»

It was narrated by Muslim (no. 2593) with the wording,

> «O 'Â'ishah! surely Allah is gentle; He loves gentleness and gives due to gentleness what He does not give due to harshness and what He does not give due to what is equivalent to it.»

In his *Ṣaḥîḥ* (no. 2594), Muslim narrated from 'Â'ishah رضي الله عنها, from the Prophet ﷺ [who] said,

> «Surely, gentleness does not exist in anything except that it beautifies it and it is not removed from anything except that it disfigures it.»

Muslim also narrated (no. 2592) from Jarîr bin 'Abdillah رضي الله عنه from the Prophet ﷺ [who] said,

> «Whoever forbids gentleness, he forbids good.»

Allah had commanded the two noble Prophets, Mūsâ ﵇ and Hârūn ﵇, to invite Pharaoh with gentleness and lenience, for He said,

﴿ ٱذْهَبَآ إِلَىٰ فِرْعَوْنَ إِنَّهُۥ طَغَىٰ ۝ فَقُولَا لَهُۥ قَوْلًا لَّيِّنًا لَّعَلَّهُۥ يَتَذَكَّرُ أَوْ يَخْشَىٰ ﴾

(Go to Pharaoh. Surely, he has transgressed. Then make a lenient statement to him, perhaps he will remember or fear [Me]) (20:43-44).

Allah described the noble Companions with the compassion in what is between them, for He said,

﴿ مُّحَمَّدٌ رَّسُولُ ٱللَّهِ ۚ وَٱلَّذِينَ مَعَهُۥٓ أَشِدَّآءُ عَلَى ٱلْكُفَّارِ رُحَمَآءُ بَيْنَهُمْ ۖ ﴾

(Muḥammad is Allah's Messenger and those who are with him stern against the disbelievers and merciful between themselves) (48:29).

The People of the Sunnah's Stance on the Scholar When He Errs is that He is Excused. Thus, He is Not Hereticated, Nor is He Boycotted

Infallibility is not for anyone after Allah's Messenger ﷺ, so no scholar is safe from errors. Whoever errs should not be followed in his error, and that error should not be taken as a means to disgrace him and caution against him. Rather, his few errors should be forgiven because of the many [things he is] correct [in]. Whoever was from these scholars who have passed, then one should benefit from his knowledge with the wariness of following him in the error, supplicating for him and asking [Allah to have] mercy upon him. And whoever was alive, whether he was a scholar or a student of knowledge, he is to be informed of his error with gentleness, lenience, and love for his well-being from the error and his return to [what is] correct.

Imams al-Baihaqî, an-Nawawî, and Ibn Ḥajar al-'Asqalânî are from the scholars who have passed while having defectiveness in the issues of creed and the scholars and the students of knowledge cannot do without their knowledge—nay, surely their writings are from the important references for those who busy themselves with knowledge.

So as for Imam Aḥmad bin Ḥusain, Abū Bakr al-Baihaqî, then surely, in *as-Siyar* (18/163 and what is after it), regarding him, adh-Dhahabî said, "He is the ḥafiḍḥ, the 'allâmah, the credible, the jurist, Shaikh of Islam." He said, "It was blessed for him in his knowledge and he composed beneficial works." He said, "He withdrew within his village devoting himself with compiling and writing. So he worked on *as-Sunan al-Kabîr* in ten volumes and no one has similar to it." He mentioned that he had many other books and his book *as-Sunan al-Kubrâ* was printed in ten large volumes. He conveyed words from Ḥâfiḍḥ 'Abdil-Ghâfir bin Ismâ'îl [who] said regarding him, "His writings come close to a thousand volumes, of which no one had preceded him to. He combined between the knowledge of Ḥadîth, jurisprudence, the clarifying of the defects of Ḥadîth, and the aspect of the combining between[51] the ḥadîths." adh-Dhahabî also said, "So the works of al-Baihaqî are of great worth, ample in benefits. Few were those who mastered their works like Imâm Abî Bakr, so it is necessary for the scholar to give attention to these, especially his *Sunan al-Kubrâ*."

As for Imam Yaḥyâ bin Sharaf an-Nawawî, then in *Tadhkirah al-Ḥuffâḍḥ* (4/359), regarding him, adh-Dhahabî had said, "The imam, the ḥâfiḍḥ, the unique, the exemplar, Shaikh of Islam, the star of the Patrons[52] ... author of beneficial works." He said,

> Along with what he was upon of the battle with his soul, the implementation of the intricacies of

---

[51] **[t]** I.e., reconciling seemingly contradictory authentic narrations.

[52] **[t]** Ar. awliyâ' (أولياء) (sing. walî (ولي)) – helper, supporter, benefactor, sponsor; friend, close associate; patron, protector; legal guardian; saint.

> piety[53] and control, the filtering of the soul from flaws and erasing it from its inclinations, he was a memorizer of the Ḥadîth, its sciences, its men, its authentic and its defective; [he was] at the head in knowledge of the [body of] opinion.

In *al-Bidâyah wan-Nihâyah* (17/540), Ibn Kathîr said,

> Then he took great care in composing and he gathered many things. From them is what he completed and from them is what he did not complete. From what he completed were *Sharḥ Muslim,*[54] *ar-Rawdah,*[55] *al-Minhâj,*[56] *ar-Riyâḍ,*[57] *al-Adhkâr, at-Tibyân, Taḥrîr at-Tanbîh*[58] and its authentication, *Tahdhîb al-Asmâ' wal-Lughât, Ṭabaqât al-Fuqahâ'*, and other than that. From what he did not complete—and if completed, it would not have an equal in its matter—is *al-Muhaddhab*'s explanation, which he called *al-Majmū'*. He reached until the book of usury in it and excelled in it,[59] mastered and caused benefit, and he criticised accurately. He edited the jurisprudence of the [Shâfi'î body of] opinion and other [bodies of opinion] in it. He edited the Ḥadîth according to what is befitting, the rare [words], the language, and important things only found in it ... I do not

53 **[t]** Ar. wara' (ورع) – piety, piousness, godliness; caution, cautiousness; reserve.
54 **[t]** I.e., *al-Minhâj Sharḥ Muslim bin al-Ḥajjâj.*
55 **[t]** I.e., *Rawḍah aṭ-Ṭâlibîn.*
56 **[t]** I.e., *Daqâ'iq al-Minhâj.*
57 **[t]** I.e., *Riyâḍ aṣ-Ṣâliḥîn.*
58 **[t]** I.e., *Taḥrîr Alfâḍh at-Tanbîh aw Lughah al-Fiqh.*
59 **[t]** I.e., he excelled in his explanation of *al-Muhaddab.*

> know better than it regarding the books of jurisprudence.

With this vastness and mastery in writings, he was not from those who lived long, for the period of his life was forty-five years; he was born 731H and died 676H.

As for Ḥâfiḍh Aḥmad bin 'Alî bin Ḥajar al-'Asqalânî, then he is the imam famous for his many writings. The most important of them is *Fat·ḥ al-Bârî Sharḥ Ṣaḥîḥ al-Bukhârî*, which is a great reference work for the scholars. [Also] from them are *al-Iṣâbah,*[60] *Tahdhîb at-Tahdhîb* and his *Taqrîb,*[61] *Lisân al-Mîzân, Ta'jîl al-Manfa'ah,*[62] *Bulūgh al-Marâm*, and others.

From the contemporaries is the shaikh, the 'allâmah, the traditionist[63] Muḥammad Nâṣir ad-Dîn al-Albânî. I do not know of a counterpart for him in this era with regards to meticulousness in Ḥadîth and vastness of familiarity in it. He was not safe from falling in matters considered by many to be errors from him, like his concern with the issue of the ḥijâb and the stipulating that veiling the woman's face is not an obligation, but a desirable [act].[64] If what he said was true, then it surely is from the truth whose concealment is necessary, because of some of the women who desire unveiling depending on it. Like that is his statement, "Surely, placing the [two] hands on the chest after the bowing[65] is a misguiding heresy," in the

---

[60] **[t]** I.e., *al-Iṣâbah fî Tamayyuz aṣ-Ṣaḥâbah.*

[61] **[t]** I.e., *Taqrîb at-Tahdhîb.*

[62] **[t]** I.e., *Ta'jîl al-Manfa'ah bi Zawâ'id Rijâl al-A'immah al-Arba'ah.*

[63] **[t]** Ar. muḥaddith (مُحَدِّث) – speaker, transmitter of Prophetic statements and traditions. In Islamic terminology it refers to a scholar of the branches of knowledge pertaining to Prophetic narrations and traditions, referred to by some Orientalist scholars as a 'traditionist', hence my use of it here.

[64] **[t]** Ar. mustaḥabb (مُستَحَب) – recommended, commendable, desirable; well-liked.

[65] **[t]** Ar. rukū' (رُكُوع) – bowing (at the waist, especially in prayer).

book, *Ṣifah aṣ-Ṣalâh an-Nabî* ﷺ, while it is a disputed issue. Like that is what he mentioned in *Silsilah aḍ-Ḍa'îfah* (no. 2355), namely that the lack of taking from what exceeds the fistful of the beard is from the incidental heresies. And like that is his forbidding circular gold for women. And with my disapproval of his statement in these issues, I surely cannot do without—and I see that others cannot do without—his books and the benefit from them. How excellent is the statement of Imam Mâlik رحمه الله, "Everything is taken or rejected from one's statements, except the companion of this grave," and he pointed to the grave of the Prophet ﷺ.

These are transmissions from a group from the People of Knowledge in stipulation and elucidation of forgiving the scholar's error with regard to the many [things he is] correct [in]:

Sa'îd bin al-Musayyib (d.93H) said, "It is not from a scholar, nor a distinguished [person], nor a virtuous [person], except he has a fault. Whoever's virtue was more than his deficiency, however, his deficiency goes away because of his virtue just as whoever's deficiency overwhelmed him, his virtue goes away." Others said, "The scholar is not safe from error. So whoever scarcely erred and was often correct, then he is a scholar, while whoever was scarcely correct and often erred, then he is an ignorant [person]."[66]

'Abdullah bin al-Mubârak (d.181H) said, "If the man's merits outweighed his drawbacks, do not mention the drawbacks. And if the drawbacks outweighed the merits, do not mention the merits."[67]

---

[66] *Jâmi' Bayân al-'Ilm wa Faḍlih* by Ibn 'Abdil-Barr, (2/48).
[67] *Siyar A'lâm an-Nubalâ'* by adh-Dhahabî, (8/352, 1st ed.).

Imâm Aḥmad (d.241H) said, "The likes of Is·ḥâq (i.e., Ibn Râhawaih) have not crossed the bridge from Khurasân even though he differed with us in things, for surely, the people do not cease to differ with one another."[68]

Abū Ḥâtim bin Ḥibbân (d.354H) said,

> 'Abdul-Malik—i.e., Ibn Abî Sulaimân—was from the best of the People of Kūfah and their ḥâfiḍhs. The general rule for whoever memorises and narrates from his memory is that he makes mistakes. It is not from justice to leave the Ḥadîth of a credible shaikh whose integrity is sound because of mistakes he makes in his narration. If we were to traverse this path, it would certainly necessitate us leaving the Ḥadîth of az-Zuhrî, Ibn Juraij, ath-Thawrî, and Shu'bah, because they were from the people of memorization and precision. They used to narrate from their memory and they were not infallible such that they did not make mistakes in their narrations. Rather, the precaution and the foremost in the likes of this is acceptance of what the credible [person] narrates of the narrations and leaving what is sure he is mistaken in, so long as that is not excessive from him such that it outweighs [what he is] correct [in]. For if it was like that, at that time, the leaving is deserved.[69]

Shaikh of Islam Ibn Taimiyyah (d.728H) said,

> From what should be recognized is that the groups associated to [those] followed in the fundamentals

[68] Ibid., (11/371).
[69] *ath-Thiqât*, (7/97-98).

of the religion and [theological] rhetoric are of [varying] degrees. From them are [those] who have opposed the Sunnah in great fundamentals, and from them are [those] who have certainly opposed the Sunnah in intricate matters.

Whoever might have refuted others from the groups that are further away from the Sunnah than he is, then he is praised with regards to what he refuted of the falsehood and said of the truth. He might, however, have extended beyond justice in his refutation in where he denied some of the truth and spoke some falsehood. So he might have refuted a large heresy with a heresy of lesser significance than it and refuted a falsehood with a falsehood of lesser significance than it. This is the condition of most of the People of [Theological] Rhetoric associated with the Sunnah and Congregation.

If the likes of these did not make what they innovated a saying by which they divide the congregation of Muslims, making allies and enemies according to it, it would be from a type of mistake; and Allah ﷻ forgives the believers for their mistakes in the likes of that.

Because of this, many of the predecessors and the imams of the [Muslim] nation fell into the likes of this; they had statements they made due to independent judgement,[70] [which] opposed what

[70] **[t]** Ar. ijtihâd (اجتهاد) - effort, exertion, endeavour, pains; application; independent judgement in a legal or theological question using established jurisprudential principles to derive rulings from the available texts.

> was established in the Book and the Sunnah. Contrary to [those] who ally with the one who agrees with them and make enemies of their opposers; they cause division among the congregation of Muslims; they excommunicate and declare their opposers sinners, but not those who agree with them in the issues of opinions and independent judgements; they make it lawful to fight their opposers, but not those who agree with them, for these [people] are from the people of division and differings.[71]

And he said,

> Many of the mujtahids[72] from the Predecessors and the later generations[73] have said and done what is a heresy while they did not know it was a heresy either because of weak ḥadîths they assumed were authentic, because of verses from which they understood what was not intended from them, or because of an opinion they held while texts did not reach them regarding the issue. If the man was godly to his Lord as much as he was able, he is entered into His saying,
>
> ﴿ رَبَّنَا لَا تُؤَاخِذْنَآ إِن نَّسِينَآ أَوْ أَخْطَأْنَا ﴾

---

[71] *Majmū' al-Fatâwâ*, (3/348-349).

[72] **[t]** Ar. mujtahid (مُجْتَهِد) – diligent, industrious; a legist or jurist who is capable of independent judgement (see footnote no. 70).

[73] **[t]** Ar. khalaf (خَلَف) – successor; descendant, offspring, scion. Here it refers to the later generations of the Islamic nation.

> **(Our Lord, Do not take us to account if we forget or fall into error) (2:286)**; and in the *Ṣaḥîḥ*, is that Allah said, "I have done [that]."[74]

Imam adh-Dhahabî (d.748H) said,

> Then surely, if what the formidable [scholar] from the imams of knowledge is correct in was numerous, his pursuit of the truth was known, his knowledge was vast, his intelligence was apparent, and his righteousness, his piety and his adherence were recognized, his mistakes are forgiven for him. Yes, we do not declare him astray, throw him away and forget his merits! Nor do we imitate him in his heresy and error; we hope for repentance from that for him.[75]

He also said,

> If we were to rise against an imam, hereticate him and boycott him, whenever he erred in his independent judgement in one of the issues with an error [that is] forgiven for him, certainly, no one with us would be safe—not Ibn Naṣr, not Ibn Mandah, not [those] who are greater than them. Allah is the people's guide to the truth and He is the most merciful of the merciful. So we seek refuge with Allah from desire and crudeness.[76]

And he also said,

---

[74] *Majmū' al-Fatâwâ*, (19/191-192).
[75] *Siyar A'lâm an-Nubalâ'*, (5/271).
[76] Ibid., (14/39-40).

> If [it were] that we were to ruin and hereticate everyone who erred in his independent judgement—despite validity of his faith and his aspiring to follow the truth—certainly, few [are those] from the imams who would be safe with us. May Allah have mercy upon the people by His grace and His kindness.[77]

He also said, "We love the Sunnah and its people. And we love the scholar according to what he has of adherence and praiseworthy characteristics. We do not love what he heresied with palatable interpretation. Certainly, the consideration is with the abundance of merits."[78]

Ibn al-Qayyim (d.751) said,

> Recognition of the virtue and the abilities of Islam's imams, their rights and their ranks, and that their virtue, their knowledge and their sincerity for Allah and His Messenger, does not obligate acceptance of everything they say. Whatever occurred in their verdicts from the issues in which what the Messenger came with was hidden from them, then they spoke with the extent of their knowledge, while the truth was in opposition to it, does not obligate the throwing away of their statements in totality, diminishing them and defaming them. For these two unjust extremes opposed the intent. The intent of the path is between them both, so we do not sin, nor are we infallible, - until he said, - and whoever

[77] Ibid., (14/376).
[78] Ibid., (20/46).

> has knowledge in the law and the reality knows with certainty that the honourable man who has a righteous past and good effects in Islam; and he is a position in relation to Islam and its people; there might be the lapse and the slip from him for which he is excused—rather, [he is] rewarded due to his independent judgement. Thus it is not permissible that he be followed in it, nor is it permissible that his position, his leadership and his status be voided from the Muslims' hearts.[79]

Ibn Rajab al-Ḥanbalî (d.795H) said, "Allah refuses infallibility for a book other than His Book, and the fair [person] is [the one] who forgives the few mistakes of a person because of the many [things he is] correct [in]."[80]

---

[79] *I'lâm al-Muwaqqi'în*, (3/295).
[80] *al-Qawâ'id*, pg. 3.

The Tribulation From Some of the People of the Sunnah in This Era of Disparaging and Boycotting and the Way of Safety From It

In this time, the People of the Sunnah's occupation with one another in disparaging and in cautioning has occurred. From that, division, differing, and boycotting [one another] have resulted, while [what was] appropriate—no, [what was] incumbent was good relations, compassion between themselves, and their standing as a single rank in the face of the People of Heresies and Desires, the opposers of the People of the Sunnah and Congregation. And that[81] returns to two causes:

The first of them is that from the People of the Sunnah in this era are [those] whose practice and whose chief concern is the following of errors and searching for them, whether they be in writings or tapes, then cautioning from whoever any of these errors occurred from. From these errors for which the individual is disparaged and because of which he is cautioned

[81] **[t]** I.e., the disparaging and the cautioning

against is, for example, his cooperation with one of the organisations [82] by delivering lectures or participating in conferences, while Shaikhs 'Abdul-'Azîz bin Bâz and Muḥammad bin 'Uthaimîn ﷺ had used to deliver lectures for this organisation by way of telephone. One blames it for its entering into a matter for which these two honourable scholars have given a verdict on. The person's condemnation of his own opinion is more deserving than his condemnation of the opinion of others, especially when it was an opinion for which the formidable scholars had given a verdict on. After what occurred during the treaty of al-Ḥudaibiyah, some of the companions of the Prophet ﷺ used to say, "O people, suspect the opinion with regards to the religion!"

From the disparaged are those whose benefit is tremendous, whether it be by way of lessons, writings, or sermons. He is cautioned against because he is not known to have words about so and so, or such and such group, for example. Rather, the disparaging and the cautioning has certainly reached the last remnants of some of the Arab lands, of [those] whose benefit is prevalent and their endeavours are tremendous in manifesting, spreading, and calling to the Sunnah. There is no doubt that cautioning against the likes of these contains severing the way between the students of knowledge and [those] who they can possibly benefit from with regards to knowledge and character.

The second is that from the People of the Sunnah are [those] who wrote in refutation of someone from the People of the Sunnah if he saw errors by him. Then surely, the refuted would meet the refutation with a refutation [of his own]. Then each of them would become occupied with reading what the

82 **[t]** The organisation alluded to here is Jam'iyyah Iḥyâ' at-Turâth al-Islamî, an organisation based in Kuwait dedicated to Islamic propagation around the world.

other has of writings, old or new, and likewise, listening to what he has of tapes, for the gathering of errors and the hunting of shortcomings—while it could be that some of them are by way of slip of the tongue. He turns to that by himself or others carry it out for him. Then each of them endeavours to increase the supporters he has owed by the other. Then the supporters for each one of them strive in commending the statement of whoever he supports, dispraising others, and coercing [those] who they meet to have a position on [the one] who they do not support. If he does not [take a position] he is hereticated following the heretication[83] of the other party and that is followed by his boycott. The work of these supporters for one of the two parties rebuking the other party is from the greatest of causes for the manifestation and spreading of the tribulation to a vast extent.

The affair increases in evil when both parties and the supporters for them carry out spreading what they rebuke the other for in "internet" information. Then the youth of the People of the Sunnah in the different countries—rather, the continents—become preoccupied with continually studying what is spread on the sites, which is spread by these [ones] and these [ones] of the 'it was said' and the 'he said' that does not come with any good. Rather, it comes with harm and division, of which makes these [ones] and these [ones], the supporters of each of the two parties, resemble the frequenters of the bulletin boards to inquire into what is spread on them. They also resemble [those] captivated by the athletic clubs that encourage

[83] **[t]** Ar. tabdî' (تَبْدِيع) - heretication (or heretification): to hereticate, to pronounce or denounce as heretical [or innovatory], to make a heretic [or innovator] of someone. See *Webster's Third New International Dictionary Unabridged*, 1971. vol. 2, pg. 1059.

all of them to be factions. Then the controversy, the frigidity, and the contention occur amongst them as a result of that.

The road of safety from these tribulations is in what follows:

Firstly, in what is connected with disparaging and cautioning, one should consider what follows:

1. that whoever occupies himself with disparaging and cautioning against the scholars and the students of knowledge be godly to Allah. He should be preoccupied with searching for his faults in order to escape from them instead of occupation with the faults of others. He should guard the retention of his good deeds so he does not become grieved on account of them, distributing them to whoever he afflicted with their disparagement and defamation. He is more in need of those good deeds than others on a day in which neither wealth nor children will benefit, except whoever comes to Allah with a pure heart.

2. that instead of disparaging and cautioning, one occupy himself with the acquisition of, the seriousness and the diligence in, the beneficial knowledge to make use and be useful, and [seek] benefit and [cause] benefit. So from the good the person has is that he occupies [himself] with knowledge, learning, teaching, calling [to Allah], writing. He does not occupy himself with disparaging the scholars and the students of knowledge from the People of the Sunnah, cutting off the path connected to benefiting from them, thus being from the people of destruction. If he mastered that, he would certainly be from the people of construction. The likes of this [person] occupied with disparaging does not leave behind knowledge he can make use of when he dies. With his death, the people do not

lose a scholar [who] benefits them. Rather, with his death, they are safe from his evil.

3. that the students from the People of the Sunnah in every place turn to being occupied with knowledge, with reading the useful books, and listening to the tapes by the scholars of the People of the Sunnah: the likes of Shaikh Ibn Bâz and Shaikh Ibn 'Uthaimîn, instead of their being occupied with contacting so-and-so or so-and-so, asking, “What is your view regarding so-and-so or so-and-so?” and “What do you say regarding so-and-so’s statement about so-and-so, and so-and-so’s statement about so-and-so?”

4. the students of knowledge should turn to the Presidency of the Deliverance of Verdicts for their questions about the conditions of individuals: are they[84] turned to for verdicts and the taking of knowledge, or not? It is possible for whoever has knowledge of the specific individuals to write to the Presidency of the Deliverance of Verdicts with clarification of what he knows about them for examination of that, so that when issued, the disparaging and the cautioning is issued from a direction depended on for verdicts and for clarification of who knowledge is taken from and turned to for verdicts. There is no doubt that the direction turned to for deliverance of verdicts in issues is the one that should be turned to for recognition of who verdicts are sought from and knowledge is taken from; and [there is also no doubt] that no one [should] make himself an authority in the likes of these important [matters], because from the good of the person’s Islam is his leaving what does not concern him.

---

[84] **[t]** I.e., these individuals.

Secondly, in what is connected to the refutation of whoever erred, one should consider what follows:

1. that where the error is clear and evident, the refutation be with gentleness, lenience, and a strong desire for the well-being of the mistaken [person] from the error. One should turn to Shaikh 'Abdul-'Azîz bin Bâz's ﷺ refutations to seek benefit from regarding the way in which the refutation should be.

2. if the error that is refuted contains [what is] unclear, rather, it is from the matters in which the refuter can be correct or mistaken, then he should turn to the Presidency of the Deliverance of Verdicts for the decision in that. As for when the error was clear, it is upon the refuted [person] to recant from it, because returning to the truth is better than continuance in falsehood.

3. if the refutation of another occurred from a person, he has done what is upon him. He should not occupy himself with pursuing the refuted [person]. Rather, he should be preoccupied with knowledge that brings about tremendous benefit for him and for others; this is the way of Shaikh 'Abdil-'Azîz bin Bâz ﷺ.

4. it is not permissible for any student of knowledge to test others with having a position on so-and-so, the refuted [person] or the refuter, [such that] if he agrees, he is safe and if he does not agree, he is hereticated and boycotted. It is not for anyone to ascribe the likes of this chaos in heretication and boycotting to the People of the Sunnah. It also is not for anyone to describe whoever does not traverse this chaotic way as diluting the Predecessors' methodology. The beneficial boycott among the People of the Sunnah is what benefits the boycotted [person], like the father's boycotting his son and the shaikh of his pupil. Like that is the boycott emanating from whoever has a high-ranking position and lofty standing, because a boycott [from]

the likes of these [people] is beneficial for the boycotted [person]. As for if the boycott emanated from some of the students for others, especially if it were for matters which the boycott is not tolerated, then that does not benefit the boycotted [person] in anything. Rather, the existence of frigidity, disparity, and the severance of mutual relations result from it. In words he had about Yazîd bin Mu'âwiyah in *Majmū' al-Fatâwâ* (3/413-414), Shaikh of Islam Ibn Taimiyyah said,

> The correct [position] is what the imams are upon: that he is not given love, nor is he cursed. With this then, if he were a sinner or an oppressor, then Allah forgives the sinner and the oppressor, especially if he came with tremendous good deeds. In his *Ṣaḥîḥ*, al-Bukhârî had narrated from Ibn 'Umar 🙵 that the Prophet 🙵 said, «The first army to invade Constantinople is forgiven,»[85] and the commander of the first army to invade it was Yazîd bin Mu'âwiyah, and Abū Ayūb al-Anṣârî 🙵 was with him ... .
>
> So the obligation is [adopting a] middle course in that and turning away from mention of Yazîd bin Mu'âwiyah, **testing the Muslims by him,** because this is from the heresies opposing the People of the Sunnah.

---

[85] [t] Shaikh of Islam Ibn Taimiyyah 🙵 was known to quote ḥadîths from memory and it seems that he has done so with this passage. As far as I am able to ascertain, this ḥadîth is not found in *Ṣaḥîḥ al-Bukhârî* with this wording. The closest I was able to find was ḥadîth no. 2924, in which Khâlid bin Ma'dân related from Umm Ḥarâm that the Prophet 🙵 said, «The first army from my nation to invade Caesar's city is forgiven,» and Allah is more knowledgeable.

He said, "Likewise is [causing] division among the [Muslim] nation and testing it with what Allah and His Messenger ﷺ did not command."[86]

He said,

> It is not for anyone to appoint a person other than the Prophet ﷺ for the [Muslim] nation, calling to his way, making allies and showing enmity on account of it. Nor should he appoint words for them other than the words of Allah and His Messenger, and whatever the [Muslim] nation has of, making allies and showing enmity on account of them. Rather, this is from the actions of the People of Heresies who appoint a person or words for them by which they differentiate between the [Muslim] nation and by which they make allies and enemies according to those words or that connection.[87]

And he said,

> So if the instructor or the professor had ordered the boycott, the abandonment, the dropping, or the isolation of a person, or similar to that, then it is to be looked into: for if he had committed a legitimate sin, he is penalized according to his sin without addition. If he did not commit a legitimate sin, it is not permissible that he be penalized with anything on account of the prejudice of the instructor or other than him.

---

[86] *Majmū' al-Fatâwâ*, (3/415).

[87] Ibid., (20/164).

> It is not for the instructors to rally the people and do what casts enmity and hatred between them. Rather, they should be like brothers cooperating upon reverence and godliness, just as Allah, exalted is He, said,
>
> ﴿ وَتَعَاوَنُوا۟ عَلَى ٱلْبِرِّ وَٱلتَّقْوَىٰ ۖ وَلَا تَعَاوَنُوا۟ عَلَى ٱلْإِثْمِ وَٱلْعُدْوَٰنِ ۚ ﴾
>
> **(And cooperate upon reverence and godliness and do not cooperate upon offence and transgression) (5:2).**[88]

In explanation of the ḥadîth «From the good of the person's Islam is his leaving what does not concern him,» from his book, *Jâmi' al-'Ulūm wal-Ḥikam* (1/288), Ḥâfiḍḥ Ibn Rajab said,

> This ḥadîth is a tremendous foundation from the foundations of manners. Imam Abū 'Amr bin aṣ-Ṣalâḥ related from Abî Muḥammad bin Abî Zaid, the imam of the Mâlikîs of his time, that he said, "The total of good's manners and reins branches from four ḥâdîths: the Prophet's ﷺ statement, «Whoever believed in Allah and the Last Day, then let him speak good or let him remain silent,» his ﷺ statement, « From the good of the person's Islam is his leaving what does not concern him,» his ﷺ statement to the one he summarized the counsel for, «Do not get angry,» and his ﷺ statement, «The believer wants for his brother what he wants for himself.»

[88] Ibid., (28/15-16).

I say how in need are the students of knowledge of guiding [themselves] with these manners that return with good and benefit, for them and for others, along with remoteness from harshness and crudeness, which does not bear fruit except loneliness, separation, [mutual] aversion of the hearts, and tearing of the unity.

5. upon every student of knowledge sincere to himself is that he avoid following up what is spread in internet information, from what these [people] say regarding these [people], and these [people] regarding these [people]; and when using the internet, attention to looking at the likes of Shaikh 'Abdul-'Azîz bin Bâz's ﷺ site, reading his researches and his verdicts (which have now reached twenty-one volumes), and the verdicts of the Permanent Committee (which have now reached twenty volumes). And like that, Shaikh Muḥammad bin 'Uthaimîn's ﷺ site, reading his books and his many extensive verdicts.

In conclusion, I advise the students of knowledge to thank Allah ﷻ for His granting success to them, since He made them from its[89] students; to be concerned with sincerity in seeking it and make every conceivable sacrifice for its attainment; to preserve the time by being occupied with it, because knowledge is not acquired by hoping and by remaining lazy and sluggish. Yaḥyâ bin Abî Kathîr al-Yamâmî had said, "Knowledge is not possible with the body's rest."[90] Verses have come in Allah's book and ḥadîths in His Prophet's ﷺ sunnah indicating the nobility of knowledge and the virtue of its people, like His statement, exalted is He,

---

[89] **[t]** I.e., knowledge's students.

[90] Narrated by Muslim in his *Ṣaḥîḥ* with his chain [of transmission] to him in his citing the ḥadîths of the times of the prayer.

﴿ شَهِدَ ٱللَّهُ أَنَّهُۥ لَآ إِلَٰهَ إِلَّا هُوَ وَٱلْمَلَٰٓئِكَةُ ﴾

(Allah, the angels and those given knowledge testified that there is no god [worthy of worship] except Him) (3:18)

His statement,

﴿ قُلْ هَلْ يَسْتَوِى ٱلَّذِينَ يَعْلَمُونَ وَٱلَّذِينَ لَا يَعْلَمُونَ ﴾

(Say: are those who know and those who do not know equal?) (39:9),

His statement,

﴿ يَرْفَعِ ٱللَّهُ ٱلَّذِينَ ءَامَنُوا۟ مِنكُمْ وَٱلَّذِينَ أُوتُوا۟ ٱلْعِلْمَ دَرَجَٰتٍ ﴾

(Allah raises those of you who believed and those given knowledge in degrees) (58:11),

And His statement,

﴿ وَقُل رَّبِّ زِدْنِى عِلْمًا ﴾

(And say: [my] Lord, increase me in knowledge) (20:114).

As for the ḥâdîths regarding that, then from them is his ﷺ statement, «Whoever Allah desires good for, He instructs him in the religion,»[91] his ﷺ statement, «The best of you is whoever

---

[91] It was related by al-Bukhârî (no. 71) and Muslim (no. 1037). The ḥadîth indicates that from the signs of Allah's desiring good for the servant is that He, exalted is He, instructs

learns the Qur'an and teaches it,»[92] his ﷺ statement, «Surely, with this Book Allah raises peoples and humbles others,»[93] his ﷺ statement, «Allah makes a person who heard my statement, then retained it [to memory] and conveyed it just as he heard it, shine,»[94] his ﷺ statement,

> «Whoever follows a way in which he seeks knowledge, Allah ﷻ will clear a way from the ways of Jannah because of it. Surely, the Angels humble their wings in approval for the student of knowledge. And surely, whoever is in the heavens, whoever is on the earth, and the creatures within the sea certainly seek forgiveness for the scholar. Surely, the scholar's virtue over the worshipper is like the virtue of the moon on the night of al-Badr over the rest of the stars. Surely, the scholars are the inheritors of the Prophets; surely the Prophets do not leave behind any dînârs or dirhams, but they leave behind knowledge. So whoever has received it has received an abundant fortune,»[95]

His ﷺ statement, «When the person dies his actions are cut off from him, except from three: except from recurring charity,

him in the religion, because surely, through his comprehension in the religion, he worships Allah upon insight and he calls others upon insight.

[92] It was narrated by al-Bukhârî (no. 5027).

[93] It was narrated by Muslim (no. 817).

[94] It is a recurrently narrated (Ar. mutawâtir (مُتَوَاتِر)) ḥadîth, coming from more than ten Companions. I mentioned their narrations in my book, *Dirâsah Ḥadîth «Naḍḍarallah Imra'an Sami'a Maqâlatî» Riwâyatan wa Dirâyatan.*

[95] It is a good (Ar. ḥasan (حَسَن)) ḥadîth because of other [narrations that strengthen it]. It was related by Abū Dâwud (no. 3628) and others. See its extraction in *Ṣaḥîḥ at-Targhîb wat-Tarhîb* (no. 70) and *at-Ta'lîq 'alâ Musnad al-Imam Aḥmad* (no. 21715). Ḥâfiḍh Ibn Rajab has explained this ḥadîth in a single volume, and the first sentence came in a ḥadîth in *Ṣaḥîḥ Muslim* (no. 2699).

knowledge [that] is put to use, or a righteous child who supplicates for him,»[96] his ﷺ statement,

> «Whoever called to guidance will have the likes of the rewards of whoever followed him from the reward, that not diminishing anything from their rewards. And whoever called to misguidance will have upon him the likes of the offences of whoever followed him from the offence, that not diminishing anything from their offences.»[97]

I also advise the people to preserve the time and structure it for what returns with good for the person, because of his ﷺ statement, «Two graces in which many of the people are cheated: good health and free time.»[98]

I advise being distracted from what does not concern by what does concern, because of his ﷺ statement, «From the good of the person's Islam is his leaving what does not concern him."[99]

I advise moderation and the middle course between exaggeration, harshness, excess, and negligence, because of his ﷺ statement, «Beware of exaggeration in the religion, because

---

[96] It was narrated by Muslim (no. 1631).

[97] It was related by Muslim (no. 2674).

[98] It was narrated by al-Bukhârî in his *Ṣaḥîḥ* (no. 6412) and it is the first ḥadîth he has in *Kitâb ar-Riqâq*. In this book (11/235 with *al-Fat·ḥ*), he had mentioned a narration from 'Alî bin Abî Ṭâlib ؓ [who] said, "The worldly [life] has set out from behind, and the Afterlife has set out in front; each one of them has children. So be from the children of the Afterlife, and not from the children of the worldly [life], because today is deed without reckoning, while tomorrow is reckoning without action."

[99] A good ḥadîth narrated by at-Tirmidhî (no. 2317) and others, and it is ḥadîth no. 12 from an-Nawawî's *al-Arba'în*.

whoever was before you was destroyed on account of exaggeration in religion.»[100]

And I advise caution from oppression, because of the holy ḥadîth,[101] «O my servants, I have surely forbidden oppression for Myself and I have made it forbidden among you. So do not oppress [one another],»[102] and because of his ﷺ statement, «Be god-fearing of oppression, for surely, oppression is darknesses on the Day of Standing.»[103]

I ask Allah ﷻ to grant success to the people in what contains the attainment of beneficial knowledge, acting on it, and calling to it upon insight; to unite them upon the truth and guidance, protecting them from tribulations—what is apparent from them and what is hidden. Surely, He is the Patron of that and the [One] capable of it. May Allah send salutations, peace, and blessings upon His servant and Messenger, our Prophet Muḥammad, upon his family, his Companions and whoever followed them in excellence until the Day of Reward.

---

[100] It is an authentic ḥadîth related by an-Nasâ'î and others; it is from the ḥâdîths of the Farewell Ḥajj. See its extraction in *as-Silsilah aṣ-Ṣaḥîḥah* by al-Albânî (no. 1283).
[101] **[t]** Ar. ḥadîth qudsî (حَدِيث قُدْسِي) – lit. holy or sacred ḥadîth. It refers to a ḥadîth "narrated by the Prophet ﷺ from his Lord ﷻ." See Ibn 'Uthaimîn's *Muṣ·ṭalaḥ al-Ḥadîth*.
[102] It was narrated by Muslim (no. 2577).
[103] It was narrated by Muslim (no. 2578).

The following two subjects are written down at the end of the treatise, *al-Ḥathth 'alâ Ittibâ' as-Sunnah wat-Taḥdhîr min al-Bida' wa Bayân Khaṭarihâ*, and I have considered writing them down here in order to attach them to the treatise, *Rifqan Ahl as-Sunnah bi Ahl as-Sunnah.*

The Heresy of Testing the People by Individuals

From the reprehensible heresies is what occurred in this time of some of the People of the Sunnah testing others by individuals, whether the incentive for the test is harshness for a person tested by, or whether the incentive for it is [high] commendation for another person. If the test's result was in agreement with what the tester desired, he would achieve welcoming, extolment, and commendation. Otherwise, his fortune would be disparagement, heretication, boycott, and cautioning.

These are transmissions from Shaikh of Islam Ibn Taimiyyah. The first of them [is] regarding heretication in testing by individuals, because of harshness for them, while the last of them [is] regarding heretication in testing by other individuals, because of [high] commendation for them.

In words he had about Yazîd bin Mu'âwiyah in *Majmū' al-Fatâwâ* (3/413-414), Shaikh of Islam Ibn Taimiyyah said,

> The correct [position] is what the imams are upon: that he is not given love, nor is he cursed. With this then, if he were a sinner or an oppressor, then

Allah forgives the sinner and the oppressor, especially if he came with tremendous good deeds. In his *Ṣaḥīḥ*, al-Bukhârî had narrated from Ibn 'Umar ❀ that the Prophet ❀ said, «The first army to invade Constantinople is forgiven,» and the commander of the first army to invade it was Yazîd bin Mu'âwiyah, and Abū Ayūb al-Anṣârî ❀ was with him ...

So the obligation is [adopting a] middle course in that and turning away from mention of Yazîd bin Mu'âwiyah, **testing the Muslims by him**, because this is from the heresies opposing the People of the Sunnah.

He said, "Likewise is differentiating among the [Muslim] nation and testing it with what Allah and His Messenger ❀ did not command."[104]

He said,

It is not for anyone to appoint a person other than the Prophet ❀ for the [Muslim] nation, calling to his way, making allies and showing enmity on account of it. Nor should he appoint words for them other than the words of Allah and His Messenger, and whatever the [Muslim] nation has of, making allies and showing enmity on account of them. Rather, this is from the actions of the People of Heresies who appoint a person or words for them by which they differentiate between the [Muslim] nation, and by which they make allies

---

[104] *Majmū' al-Fatâwâ*, (3/415).

> and enemies according to those words or that connection.[105]

And he said,

> So if the instructor or the professor had ordered the boycott, the abandonment, the dropping, or the isolation of a person, or similar to that, then it is to be looked into: for if he had committed a legitimate sin, he is penalized according to his sin without addition. If he did not commit a legitimate sin, it is not permissible that he be penalized with anything on account of the prejudice of the instructor or other than him.
>
> It is not for the instructors to rally the people and do what casts enmity and hatred between them. Rather, they should be like brothers cooperating upon reverence and godliness, just as Allah, exalted is He, said, (And cooperate upon reverence and godliness and do not cooperate upon offence and transgression) (5:2).[106]

If testing the people by individuals were tolerated in this time to recognize who was from the People of the Sunnah or other than them through this testing, certainly the most deserving and the foremost in that is Shaikh of Islam, muftî of the world, imam of the People of the Sunnah in his time, our shaikh, Shaikh 'Abdul-'Azîz bin 'Abdillah bin Bâz, who died on 28th of the month of Muḥarram in 1420H—may Allah have mercy on him, forgive him, and reward him generously. [He is] the one who all people

[105] Ibid., (20/164).
[106] Ibid., (28/15-16).

recognized for the vastness of his knowledge, the abundance of his benefit, his truthfulness, his gentleness, his tenderness, and his eagerness for the guidance and direction of the people; we consider him as such and we do not vouch for anyone over Allah. Indeed, he had a unique methodology in calling to Allah, teaching the people the good, and ordering them with the recognized [good] and prohibiting them from the reprehensible [matters]. It was characterized by gentleness and lenience in his advice and his many refutations of others; a correct methodology [that] sets the People of the Sunnah upright and does not oppose them,[107] encourages them and does not offer resistance against them, lifts them and does not scrutinize them. [It was] a methodology [that] gathers and does not separate, collects and does not rip them apart, directs them and does not scatter them, facilitates and does not make things difficult. How in need are [those] occupied with knowledge and its students of traversing this straight road and tremendous methodology

---

[107] From those who were harmed by the arrows of disparagement and resistance from some of those who demand too much (Ar. mutakallifūn (مُتَكَلِّفون)), while [having] achieved estimation, direction, and encouragement from the eminent Shaikh 'Abdil-'Azîz bin Bâz ﵀, are two noble men teaching in the Prophetic Mosque whose lessons are heard on the radio. One of the two,[i] the period of his teaching in [the Prophetic mosque] exceeds 50 years; the first time I saw him teaching in it was at the end of Ḥajj on the year 1376H. After Shaikh 'Abdul-'Azîz bin Bâz's transfer from the Presidency of the Islamic University in Madînah to the Presidency of Academic Research and Verdicts in Riyâḍ, every time I met him he ﵀ used to ask me about the lessons in the Prophetic Mosque and the teachers in it, and he would specifically ask about that noble man.

The second[ii] is occupied with knowledge and concerned with teaching; he teaches in the Prophetic Mosque, in Jeddah and Mecca. I had heard from one of the teachers in the Islamic University in Madînah that he entered Shaikh 'Abdul-'Azîz bin Bâz's ﵀ mosque in Mecca and that noble man was found giving a lesson in the presence of the eminent Shaikh 'Abdul-'Azîz bin Bâz's ﵀. When the questions regarding the lesson came, Shaikh 'Abdul-'Azîz ﵀ was entrusted with answering them. These two are examples of his estimation, direction, and encouragement for [those who] occupy [themselves] with learning knowledge.

[107i] **[t]** I.e., Shaikh Abū Bakr al-Jaza'irî.

[107ii] **[t]** I.e., Shaikh Muḥammad Mukhtâr ash-Shinqîṭî.

because of what it contains of the bringing about of good for the Muslims and the driving away of harms from them.

The obligation upon those who fell into that testing, the followers and the followed, is that they free [themselves] from this road that [has] divided the People of the Sunnah. Because of it, they showed enmity to one another. That is by the followers leaving the testing and all of whatever results from it of hatred, boycotting, and severance [of mutual relations]; by being brothers, harmonious, cooperating on reverence and godliness; and by the followed freeing [themselves] from this way upon which they were followed and publicize their liberation from it and from the deed of whoever fell into it. With that, the followers are safe from this trial and the followed from the consequence of being followed in this testing and what results from it of harm returning to them and to others.

Cautioning Against the Tribulation From Some of the People of the Sunnah in This Era of Disparaging and Heretication

Close to the heresy of testing the people by individuals is what occurred during this time of a small band from the People of the Sunnah's infatuation with the disparaging and the heretication of some of their brothers from the People of the Sunnah and what resulted from that of boycotting, severance [of mutual relations] between them, and cutting off the path of [deriving] benefit from them. From that disparaging and heretication is what was built upon the assumption that what is not a heresy is a heresy. From the examples of that is that the two honourable shaikhs, 'Abdul-'Azîz bin Bâz ﷺ and Ibn 'Uthaimîn ﷺ had delivered a verdict for a group's participation in a matter, [as] they saw the benefit in that participation.[108] From [those] that [this group given] the verdict did not arouse admiration in was that small band, for it reprimanded that

[108] **[t]** See footnote no. 82.

group because of that.[109] The matter did not stop at this extent. Rather, the blame transferred to whoever cooperated with it by delivering lectures. He would be described as a diluter of the methodology of the Predecessors—despite [the fact] that these two honourable shaikhs used to deliver lectures to this group by way of telephone.

Also from that is the occurrence of cautioning against attending a person's lessons because he does not speak about such-and-such person or such-and-such group; a person from my pupils at the Faculty of [Islamic] Law at the Islamic University[110] has undertaken the bulk of that. He graduated from it in 1395-1396H and his ranking was 104th from his batch of the 119 graduates.[111] He is not known for being occupied with knowledge, nor do I know of him having [any] registered academic lessons, nor [any] writing regarding knowledge, small nor large. The bulk of his merchandise is disparagement, heretication, and cautioning against many [individuals] from the People of the Sunnah. This disparager does not reach the ankles of some of those he disparages because of the abundance

---

[109] **[t]** I.e, for its participation in the matter alluded to.

[110] **[t]** See footnote no. 21. Throughout this portion of his treatise, the shaikh refers to him as 'the disparager' and 'the disparaging pupil'.

[111] This information is conveyed from the books, *Khirrîjû al-Jâmi'ah min 'Âmm 1394-95 ilâ 1395-96H* and *Dalîl al-Jâmi'ah al-Islamiyyah li-'Âmm 1395-1396H.* Both had been printed during the time which I was the first functionary at the Islamic University. Both contain a foreword from me and are found in my library.

In one of his tapes, for which there is no halter, nor bridle, negation of his being one of my pupils and that he does not remember me entering upon them in the class except for a single time during a waiting period has occurred from this disparaging pupil!!! From the amazing [things] is his recollection of the claimed waiting period and his forgetfulness—or his [feigning] forgetfulness—of the weekly period for jurisprudence during the course of the whole academic year!! At that time, I was doing administrative work in the University. I would attend two lectures in two academic classes during one of the days of the week, then I would return to my administrative work; I did not have any waiting periods. His many colleagues, of the 118 graduates, know this reality and are not ignorant of it.

of their benefit in their lessons, their lectures, and their writings. The amazement does not cease if a sensible person heard a tape he has containing a recording of a long telephone conversation between Madînah and Algeria. The questioned eats the flesh of many from the People of the Sunnah in it, while the questioner squanders his wealth without right. In this tape, the number of [those] asked about may add up to thirty individuals: among them the minister, the old and the young, and among them a small band not mourned! Whoever was not asked about in this tape may have been saved from it, while some of those who were saved from it were not saved from other tapes he has, which the internet information includes. The obligation upon him is restraint from eating the flesh of the scholars and students of knowledge. The obligation upon the youth and the students of knowledge is that they do not incline towards those disparagements and heretications that harm and do not benefit and that they occupy [themselves] with beneficial knowledge that returns to them with a good and praiseworthy outcome in this world and the Hereafter. In his book, *Tabyîn Kadhib al-Muftarî* (pg. 29), Ḥâfiḍh Ibn 'Âsâkir ﷺ had said,

> And know—O my brother, may Allah grant us and you success to His pleasure and may He make us from those who dread Him and are godly to Him with the deserved godliness to Him—that the flesh of the scholars, may Allah's mercy be upon them, is poisonous and Allah's custom with regards to tearing the curtains from their shortcomings is known.

In my treatise, *Rifqan Ahl as-Sunnah bi Ahl as-Sunnah*, I had mentioned a large sum of verses, ḥadîths, and narrations, regarding guarding the tongue against backbiting the People of the Sunnah, especially the people of knowledge among them. Despite that, this disparager was not amazed. He described it as not being fit for distribution and he cautioned against it and whoever distributed it. There is no doubt that whoever comes across this disparagement and reads the treatise will find that this ruling is in one valley while the treatise is in another and that the matter is just as the poet said,

> The eye may be denied the sun's light due to conjunctivitis,
> while the mouth is denied the taste of water due to an illness.

As for the disparaging student's statement for the treatise, *Rifqan Ahl as-Sunnah bi Ahl as-Sunnah*,

> So for example, regarding the words that Shaikh 'Abdil-'Azîz bin Bâz's methodology and Shaikh Ibn 'Uthaimîn's methodology are contrary to the methodology of other People of the Sunnah, this is a mistake—no doubt. He means they would not increase the [number of] refutations, while they would refute the opposer. If this is correct, it is contrary to the methodology of the People of the Sunnah and Congregation and, in reality, is an attack on the two shaikhs and others of whom it is possible that this speech can be said about!!!

The reply to it is from [several] aspects:

The first aspect is that it is not in the treatise that Shaikh 'Abdul-'Azîz bin Bâz ﷺ did not increase the [number of] refutations. Rather, his refutations were many. In the treatise, it has been mentioned on pg. 31,

> that where the error is clear and evident, the refutation be with gentleness, lenience, and a strong desire for the well-being of the mistaken [person] from the error. One should turn to Shaikh 'Abdul-'Azîz bin Bâz's ﷺ refutations to seek benefit from regarding the way in which the refutation should be.

The second aspect is that I did not consider mentioning Shaikh Ibn 'Uthaimîn's ﷺ methodology regarding refutations, because I do not know of writings, small or large, by him regarding refutations. I asked one of his pupils closely connected to him about that and he informed me that he did not know of anything by him of refutations; that does not defame him, because he was occupied with relating knowledge, distributing it, and writing.

The third aspect is that Shaikh 'Abdil-'Azîz bin Bâz's ﷺ methodology differed from the methodology of the disparaging student and those who resemble him, because the shaikh's methodology was characterised by gentleness, lenience, and the desire for benefiting the one being advised, helping him to the path of safety. As for the disparager and whoever resembles him, then they are characterised by severity, alienation, and cautioning. Many of those whose disparagement is in his tapes were commended and called to by Shaikh 'Abdul-'Azîz. He would urge them upon calling [to Allah] and teaching the people and he would urge upon benefiting from them and taking [knowledge] from them.

In short, I did not attribute the lack of refutation of others to Shaikh 'Abdil-'Azîz bin Bâz ﷺ. As for Ibn 'Uthaimîn, then I did not turn [my attention] to him with [any] mention regarding the affair of refutations. What the disparager mentioned does not correspond to what is in the treatise and it is the clearest of evidences for his stumbles and his lack of verification. If this was from him in written words, then how is the situation for which there is no writing?!

As for the statement of the treatise's disparager,

> In reality, I have read the treatise and I recognized the position of the People of the Sunnah regarding it. Hopefully, you have seen the refutations from some of the scholars and shaikhs—and I do not think the refutations will stop at that. There are certainly those who will also refute, because it is just as the poet says:
>
> Shaqîq came displaying his spear;
> surely, among your cousins are spears,[112]

As such: [he wrote] 'displayer' (عارضٌ), while what is correct is 'displaying' (عارضًا).[113]

So the reply is that those who he meant by "the People of the Sunnah" are those whose methodology differs from Shaikh 'Abdil-'Azîz's ﷺ methodology, which I will point out shortly. With these words, he seeks to incite the determinations of

---

[112] **[t]** See: http://www.salafitalk.net/st/viewmessages.cfm?Forum=23&Topic=2078&srow=21&erow=40 (accessed Jan. 13, 2014).

[113] **[t]** Shaikh 'Abdul-Muḥsin is criticizing a grammar mistake Shaikh Fâliḥ al-Ḥarbî made in the original Arabic for this line of poetry: he wrote the word 'âriḍ (عارض) in the nominative case when he should have written it in the accusative case (عارضًا). I have translated the line according to its proper meaning as otherwise, it would not have made sense.

whoever does not know them to discredit the treatise after he incited whoever knows them. In reality, I did not display a spear. On the contrary, I offered an advice, of which the disparager and whoever resembles him did not accept, because the advice for the advised resembles the remedy for the disease. From the ailing are those who use the remedy even if it was bitter because of what is hoped of [some] benefit, while from the advised are those who are turned away from the advice by desire, not accepting it. Rather, they caution against it. I ask Allah to grant the people success, guidance, and security from the devil's deception and deceit.

Three [people] have joined the disparaging student: two in Makkah and Madînah,[114] both from my students in the Islamic University in Madînah. The first of them graduated in 1384-1385H and the second in 1391-1392H. As for the third,[115] then [he is] in the extreme south of the country. The second and the third have described whoever distributes the treatise as being a heretic[116] and this is wholesale and general heretication. I do not know or not if they know that it is distributed by the scholars and students who are not characterized by [any] heresy. I expect to be supplied with the observations from them upon which they built this general heretication—if they exist—for further examination.

Shaikh 'Abdur-Rahman as-Sudais, the imam and preacher of the Sacred Mosque, has a sermon [which was] delivered from the Sacred Mosque's pulpit. In it, he cautioned against the

---

[114] **[t]** I.e., Shaikhs Rabî' bin Hâdî al-Madkhalî and 'Ubaid bin 'Abdillah al-Jâbirî, respectively.

[115] **[t]** I.e., Shaikh Aḥmad bin Yaḥyâ an-Najmî.

[116] **[t]** See the same URL as found in footnote no. 112 to find these statements by Shaikhs 'Ubaid and Aḥmad.

People of the Sunnah's battling one another. We should turn the sights to it, for surely it is important and useful.

I ask Allah ﷻ that He grant the people success for what He is pleased with, for comprehension of the religion, firmness upon the truth, and distraction from what does not concern by what concerns. Surely, He is the Patron of that and the [One] capable of it. May Allah send salutations, peace, and blessings upon our Prophet Muhammad, upon his family and companions.

Appendix

Once Again, Gentleness, O People of the Sunnah, With the People of the Sunnah

The praise is for Allah, there is no movement nor power except with Allah, and may Allah send salutations, peace, and blessings upon His slave and His Messenger, our Prophet Muḥammad, and upon his family, his companions, and whoever was a supporter of his.

As for what follows, then surely, [those] occupied with legal knowledge from the People of the Sunnah and Congregation, [those] going by what the predecessors of the [Muslim] nation were upon, in this era, are in greater need of camaraderie and giving sincere advice regarding what is between them, especially while they are a small minority in comparison to the sects and parties [that] deviated from what the predecessors of the [Muslim] nation were upon. More than ten years ago and during the last [days] of the time of the two lofty shaikhs, our shaikh, Shaikh 'Abdul-'Azîz bin Bâz and Shaikh Muḥammad bin 'Uthaimîn, may Allah have mercy on them, a very small band from the People of the Sunnah turned to [being] occupied with cautioning against some of the parties opposed to what the predecessors of the [Muslim] nation were upon—a deed praised and thanked.

The regretable [thing], however, is that after the deaths of the two shaikhs, some of this troop turned to the derogation of some of their brothers from the People of the Sunnah, [both] within the country[117] and abroad, those calling to sticking to what the predecessors of the [Muslim] nation were upon. It was from their right upon them to accept and support their [performance of] good deeds and to straighten them out in regards to what occurs from them of error if it were established that it was an error, then not occupy themselves with furnishing their sittings with mentioning them and cautioning against them. Rather, they should occupy themselves with knowledge—studying [it], teaching [it], and inviting [to it]. This is the proper methodology for improvement and reparation that our shaikh, Shaikh 'Abdul-'Azîz bin Bâz ﷲ, the imam of the People of the Sunnah and the Congregation of this era was upon. [Those] occupied with knowledge in this era are few and are in need of growth, not of diminishment; of camaraderie, not severance [of mutual relations]; the likes of what the grammarians said can be said about them: "the diminutive[118] cannot be made smaller." In *Majmū' al-Fatâwâ*, Shaikh of Islam said,

> ... and you know that from the tremendous principles that are [from][119] the collection of the religion: are union of the hearts, gathering of the

---

[117] **[t]** I.e., within Saudi Arabia.
[118] **[t]** I.e., the diminutive form of a word; e.g., kutaib (كُتَيّب – meaning booklette or small book) is the diminutive form of the word kitâb (كِتَاب – book).
[119] **[t]** This word is omitted from al-'Abbâd's quote, but is found in the original text.

word, and reparation of disagreements, for surely, Allah, exalted is He, says,

﴿ فَٱتَّقُواْ ٱللَّهَ وَأَصۡلِحُواْ ذَاتَ بَيۡنِكُمۡۖ ﴾

(So be godly to Allah and mend your disagreements,)[120]

He says,

﴿ وَٱعۡتَصِمُواْ بِحَبۡلِ ٱللَّهِ جَمِيعٗا وَلَا تَفَرَّقُواْۚ ﴾

(and collectively cling to Allah's rope and do not divide,)[121]

He says,

﴿ وَلَا تَكُونُواْ كَٱلَّذِينَ تَفَرَّقُواْ وَٱخۡتَلَفُواْ مِنۢ بَعۡدِ مَا جَآءَهُمُ ٱلۡبَيِّنَٰتُۚ وَأُوْلَٰٓئِكَ لَهُمۡ عَذَابٌ عَظِيمٞ ﴾

(and do not be like those who divided and differed after the clear signs came to them; and those, they will have a tremendous punishment,)[122]

and the likes of that from the texts that order congregation and harmony and prohibit division and differing. The people of this foundation are the People of the Congregation, just as those outside it are the People of Division.[123]

---

[120] **[t]** Qur'an, 8:1.
[121] **[t]** Qur'an, 3:103.
[122] **[t]** Qur'an, 3:105.
[123] *Majmū' al-Fatâwâ*, vol. 28, pg. 51.

I had written a treatise about this topic with the title *Gentleness, O People of the Sunnah with the People of the Sunnah*. It was printed in the year 1424H, then [its 2nd edition] in the year 1427H. It was then printed among the compilation of my books and treatises in the year 1428.[124] I mentioned many [things] from the texts of the Book, the Sunnah, and the statements of the researching scholars from the People of the Sunnah. After the introduction, the treatise included the following topics: The Grace of [Articulated] Speech and Clarification; Preserving the Tongue from Speech Except in Good; Assumption and Spying; Gentleness and Lenience; The People of the Sunnah's Stance on the Scholar When He Errs is that He is Excused. Thus, He is Not Hereticated, Nor is He Boycotted; The Tribulation From Some of the People of the Sunnah in This Era of Disparaging and Boycotting and the Way of Safety From It; The Heresy of Testing the People by Individuals; Cautioning Against the Tribulation From Some of the People of the Sunnah in This Era of Disparaging and Heretication.

From what one regrets is that recently it has been made even worse[125] with the targeting[126] of some of the People of the Sunnah with disparagement, heretication, and what follows that of deserting [one another]. Then the questions repeat: What is your view regarding so and so hereticating so and so? Should I read such-and-such book by so-and-so who so-and-so hereticated? Some of the young students will say to [others] similar to them, "What is your stance on so and so who so and so hereticated? You simply must have a stance on him, otherwise

[124] *Kutub wa Rasâ'il 'Abdil-Muḥsin bin Ḥamad al-'Abbâd al-Badr*, vol. 6, pgs. 281-327.
[125] **[t]** Ar. ḥaṣal ziyâdah aṭ-ṭîn billatan (حصل زيادة الطين بلّةً) – lit. the clay's increase in moisture occurred.
[126] **[t]** Ar. tawjîh as-sihâm li (توجيه السهام ل) – lit. the aiming of arrows at.

we will abandon you!!!" What compounds the matter in evil is that this occurs in some of the European countries and similar to them, which have in them students from the People of the Sunnah whose wares are scant and who are in severe need of attaining beneficial knowledge and of safety from the tribulation of deserting [one another] because of blind adoption [of views] in disparagement. This methodology resembles the way of the Muslim Brotherhood, whose party's founder said about them, "Thus your call is more deserving of [having] the people come to it and it not coming to anyone ... since it is comprised of every good, while others are not free from deficiency."[127] He [also] said,

> Our position on the various calls which prevailed in this era, divided the hearts and troubled the thoughts is that we weigh them by the scale of our call. Thus, whatever agrees with it, then welcome! And whatever differs with it, then we are free of it. We believe that our call is universal and does not leave a righteous part of any call except that it touches on it briefly and points it out!!!.[128]

From the good for these students—instead of preoccupation with this tribulation—is that they become occupied with reading useful books by the People of the Sunnah, especially the books of contemporary scholars like the verdicts of our shaikh, Shaikh 'Abdil-'Azîz bin Bâz, the verdicts of the Permanent Committee for Deliverance of Verdicts, the writings of Shaikh Ibn 'Uthaimîn, and others, for surely, with that they will attain

---

[127] al-Bannâ, Shaikh Ḥasan. *Mudhakkirât ad-Da'wah wad-Dâ'iyyah*. Dâr ash-Shihâb. pg. 232.
[128] al-Bannâ, Shaikh Ḥasan. *Majmū'ah Risâ'il Ḥasan al-Bannâ*. Dâr ad-Da'wah, 1411H. pg. 240.

beneficial knowledge and become safe from 'it was said' and 'he said' and eating the flesh of some of the brothers from the People of the Sunnah. In *al-Jawâb al-Kâfî*, Ibn al-Qayyim said,

> It is astonishing that restraint and reservation from eating the unlawful, oppression, fornication, stealing, drinking alcohol, looking at the forbidden, and other [such things] are easy for the human, while restraint from the movement of his tongue is difficult for him. You even see[129] a man [associated] with religion, asceticism, and worship, speaking words,[130] which he does not pay any mind to, that anger Allah. With a single word from them he descends further than what is between the east and the west. And how many men have you seen abstain from vile deeds and oppression while his tongue cuts into the honours of the living and the dead and he is unconcerned about what he says.[131]

When [both] summarized speech and elaborated speech by one of the People of the Sunnah is found, then that which is befitting is [to have] charitable assumptions of him and to take his summarized [speech] according to his elaborated [speech],[132] due to the statement of 'Umar ﷺ "Do not assume except good of

129 **[t]** The quote al-'Abbâd provides reads "even the man is seen" (حتى يُرى الرجل). This appears to be a typo; I have referred to another edition of the book and translated it accordingly.

130 **[t]** al-'Abbâd's quote has "he speaks a word that angers Allah" (يتكلم بالكلمة من سخط الله). According to the previously mentioned edition, it should be "he speaks words that anger Allah" (يتكلم بالكلمات من سخط الله).

131 *al-Jawâb al-Kâfî*, pg. 203. **[t]** See *ad-Dâ' wad-Dawâ'*, pg. 226-227 (ed. 'Alî bin Ḥasan al-Ḥalabî; Dâr Ibn al-Jawzî).

132 Here al-'Abbâd confirms one of the principles al-Ma'ribî is accused of having innovated as being a real and valid principle used by the People of the Sunnah when dealing with ambiguous statements made by others.

a word that eminated from your believing brother when you find for it a good meaning."[133] In *ar-Radd 'alal-Bakrî*, Shaikh of Islam Ibn Taimiyyah said, "[It is] known that the speaker's explanatory speech does away with his summarized and his explicit is given priority over his allusion."[134] In *aṣ-Ṣârim al-Maslūl*, he said, "The taking of the jurists' opinions from generalizations without examining what their speech explained and what their foundations necessitate leads to repulsive opinions."[135] In *al-Jawâb aṣ-Ṣaḥîḥ li Man Baddal Dîn al-Maṣîḥ*, he said, "So it is obligated that the speaker's speech be explained by his other [speech], that his speech be taken here and here,[136] and [that] the usage he means and intends by that wording when he speaks with it be recognized."[137]

[Both] the critics and the criticized do not have infallibility and not one of them is safe from deficiency or error. The search for perfection is wanted, but [one] is not forsaken for what is less than it from the good and squandered, so it is not said, "[it is] either perfection otherwise [it is] loss," or "[it is] either complete light otherwise [it is] darkness." Rather, the deficient light is to be preserved and its enhancement is to be striven for. If two or more lamps did not exist, then a single lamp is better than the darkness. And may Allah have mercy on our shaikh, Shaikh 'Abdil-'Azîz bin Bâz, who devoted his life to legal knowledge—learning [it], acting [upon it], teaching [it], and inviting [to it]—and was concerned with encouraging shaikhs

---

[133] Mentioned by Ibn Kathîr in his exegesis of Ch. al-Ḥujurât. **[t]** This footnote is part of the actual text. I have made it into a footnote to aid in the readability of the text itself. For the statement attributed to 'Umar bin al-Khaṭṭâb ﷺ, see *Tafsîr al-Qur'ân al-'Aḍhîm*, vol. 4, pg. 1756 (Mu'assasah al-Kutub ath-Thiqâfiyyah).

[134] *ar-Radd 'alal-Bakrî*, pg. 324.

[135] *aṣ-Ṣârim al-Maslūl 'alâ Shâtim ar-Rasūl*, vol. 2, pg. 512.

[136] **[t]** I.e., from various places.

[137] *al-Jawâb aṣ-Ṣaḥîḥ li Man Baddal Dîn al-Maṣîḥ*, vol. 4, pg. 44.

and students of knowledge to teach and propagate [it]. I had heard him counsel one of the shaikhs with that who gave an excuse, which the shaikh was not pleased with. He ﷺ said, "Bleariness, not blindness." The meaning [of that] is: part of [something] is not to be abandoned [merely because] the whole of it cannot be attained;[138] and if strong eyesight did not exist, but weak eyesight did, and it was bleary, then surely bleariness is better than blindness. Our shaikh ﷺ was deprived of his eyesight in the twentieth [year] of his life. However, in exchange for it Allah gave him light in insight, which he became well-known for among all the people.[139] In *Majmū' al-Fatâwâ*, Shaikh of Islam said,

> So when pure light was not extant in that [nothing] could be found except light that was not pure, otherwise the people would remain in darkness, then it is not befitting that the man find fault and prohibit from a light that contains darkness, except when a light that does not contain darkness is extant. Otherwise, how many then are [those] who turned away from that [impure light] who departed from the light entirely.[140]

This is similar to the statement of some people, "The truth is whole; it cannot be partitioned. So take it wholly, or rebuff it wholly," for surely, accepting the whole of it is true, while abandoning the whole of it is false. Whoever had with him

[138] **[t]** Ar. mâ lâ yudrak kulluh lâ yutrak ba'ḍuh (ما لا يُدرك كلّه لا يُترك بعضه) – lit. whatever the whole of it is not reached, part of it is not to be abandoned.
[139] **[t]** Ar. al-khâṣṣ wal-'âm (الخَاصّ والعَام) – lit. the special and the general.
[140] *Majmū' al-Fatâwâ*, vol. 10, pg. 364.

something of the truth is counselled to remain upon it and to strive for attainment of what is not with him of the truth.

The praised boycotting is what results in benefit, not that which results in corruption. In *Majmū' al-Fatâwâ*, Shaikh of Islam said, "If it were that whenever two Muslims differed in something they would boycott each other, there would not remain any chastity or brotherhood among the Muslims."[141] He also said,

> This boycotting differs with the boycotters' difference in their strength and their weakness, their scarceness and their abundance. For surely, the intended [goal] of it is the reprimand and discipline of the boycotted [person] and the return of the common people from the likes of his condition. So if the benefit in that were preponderant in such a manner that his boycott leads to the evil's weakening and its concealment, it would be legislated. If it were that neither the boycotted or others would be prevented by that, rather, the evil would increase and the boycotter is weak in such a manner that the corruption of that were preponderant over its benefit, the boycott is not legislated.

Until he said,

> If this is recognized, then legal abandonment is from the deeds that Allah and His Messenger ordered. So there is no escaping that obedience be sincerely for Allah and in conformity with His

[141] Ibid., vol. 28, pg. 173.

> command. Thus, [if it] is sincerely for Allah [it is] correct. So whoever boycotted [another] due to his soul's fancy or boycotted [by means of] a boycott not ordered is outside of this. And for the most part, what the souls do is what they fancy, thinking that they are doing it in obedience to Allah.[142]

The People of Knowledge have mentioned that if the scholar erred, he is not to be followed in his slip, nor is [association] from him to be disclaimed and that his slip is to be forgiven with respect to the many [things he is] correct [in]. From that is the statement of Shaikh of Islam Ibn Taimiyyah in *Majmū' al-Fatâwâ* after [some] speech preceded,

> The likes of these, if they did not make what they innovated a statement by which they divide the congregation of Islam making allies and showing enmity on account of it, it would be from the 'error' type. And Allah ﷻ forgives the believers for their mistakes in the likes of that. Due to this, many of the predecessors and imams of the [Muslim] nation fell into the likes of this: they had statements they made through an [independent] deliberation, which opposed what was established in the Book and the Sunnah, contrary to [those] who allied with the one who agreed with [them] and showed enmity for the one who opposed [them] and divided the congregation of Muslims...[143]

---

[142] Ibid., vol. 28, pgs. 206-207.
[143] Ibid., vol. 3, pg. 349.

In *Siyar A'lâm an-Nubalâ'*, adh-Dhahabî said,

> If it were that whenever an imam erred in his [independent] deliberation in a few issues—an error [that is] forgiven for him—we were to stand up against him, hereticate him and abandon him, truly none would be safe with us. Not Ibn Naṣr, not Ibn Mandah, not whoever is greater than them both. And Allah is the creation's guide to the truth, the most merciful of the merciful. So we seek refuge with Allah from desire and crudeness.[144]

He also said,

> And if it were that we relinquished and hereticated everyone who erred in his [independent] deliberation, despite the correctness of his faith and his aspiration for following the truth, [those] from the imams who would be safe with us would truly be few; may Allah have mercy on all with His gracious bestowal and His generosity.[145]

Ibn al-Jawzî mentioned that from [the instances of] disparagement is that the motive is desire. In his book *Ṣaid al-Khâṭir*, he said,

> I met shaikhs whose conditions varied. They differed in their amounts in knowledge. The most beneficial for me with respect to his companionship were [those] from them who acted on his knowledge, even if others were more knowledgeable than he. I had met a group of the

[144] *Siyar A'lâm an-Nubalâ'*, vol. 14, pgs. 39-40.
[145] Ibid., vol. 14, pgs. 376.

> scholars of Ḥadîth. They would memorise and were cognizant, but they would indulge in backbiting and set it forth as an articulation of disparagement and accreditation ... and I had certainly met 'Abdil-Wahhâb al-Anmâṭî. He was upon the canon of the Predecessors and backbiting would not be heard in his sitting ... .[146]

And in his book *Talbîs Iblîs*, he said,

> From Iblis's deceiving the companions of Ḥadîth is their defamation of one another seeking gratification [for one's thirst for revenge] and they set that forth as an articulation of the disparagement and the accreditation that the old-timers of the [Muslim] nation would use to defend the Law; and Allah is more knowledgeable of the intents.[147]

And if this were during Ibn al-Jawzî's time[148] and what was near it, then how about with the people of the 15th century?![149]

A valuable treatise has been published recently titled, *al-Ibânah 'an Kaifiyyah at-Ta'âmul Ma' al-Khilâf Bain Ahl as-Sunnah wal-Jamâ'ah,*[150] written by Shaikh Muḥammad bin 'Abdillah al-Imâm from Yemen. It had been commended by five of the shaikhs of Yemen and has included many quotes from the scholars of the People of the Sunnah, old and new, especially Shaikh of Islam

[146] *Ṣaid al-Khâṭir*, pg. 143.
[147] *Talbîs Iblîs*, vol. 2, pg. 689.
[148] [He] died in the year 597H (roughly around the year 1201CE). **[t]** This was originally part of the text.
[149] **[t]** It is currently the year 1435H.
[150] **[t]** Trans. *Illustrating How to Cooperate Despite Differences Among the People of the Sunnah and the Congregation.*

Ibn Taimiyyah and Imam Ibn al-Qayyim ﷺ, and it is an advice to the People of the Sunnah to charitably cooperate in what is between them. I have examined many of the themes of this treatise and made use of it for the indication of the places of some of the quotes that I mentioned in this address from the two imams Ibn Taimiyyah and Ibn al-Qayyim, so I recommend reading and making use of it. And how good is what he said on pg. 170 of this treatise:

> A respected [individual] may disparage some of the People of the Sunnah and then tribulations of boycotting, fragmentation, and contention break out. Fighting might break out among the People of the Sunnah themselves. So with the occurrence of something from this, it is known that the disparagement had lead to the tribulations. The obligatory [action] is to re-examine the way of disparaging and to examine the benefits and the harms, and what will cause the brotherhood to last, preserve the call, and deal with the errors. It is not proper to persist upon a way of disparagement in which harms emerge.[151]

There is not any doubt that the other shaikhs and students of knowledge from the People of the Sunnah realise what these Yemeni brothers realised, and feel pain due to this division and differing and desire to offer advice to their brothers, but the Yemeni brothers got to it first;[152] so may Allah reward them with

---

[151] *al-Ibânah 'an Kaifiyyah at-Ta'âmul Ma' al-Khilâf Bain Ahl as-Sunnah wal-Jamâ'ah*, pg. 170.

[152] **[t]** al-Imâm's book was published in 1431H (2010CE). A similar book dealing with this very issue titled *Manhaj as-Salaf aṣ-Ṣâliḥ fî Tarjîḥ al-Maṣâliḥ wa Taṭwîh al-Mafâsid wal-Qabâ'iḥ fî Uṣūl an-Naqd wal-Jarḥ wan-Naṣâ'iḥ* (trans. *The Methodology of the Righteous Predecessors in Giving Preponderance to the Benefits of Throwing Away the Harms and Abominations with*

good, and perhaps due to this advice have a share from his statement ﷺ, «Faith is Yemeni and wisdom is Yemeni.»[153] [It is] hoped that this advice from the Yemeni brothers is accepted for the purpose it was written and distributed. I do not think that anyone from the People of the Sunnah would endorse this type of disparagement and attach importance to agreeing with it while it is that which does not bear fruit except enmity and hatred between the People of the Sunnah, and roughness and hardness of the hearts.

The sensible [person's] astonishment does not cease at being in a time in which the advocates of Westernisation strive to undermine the land of the Two Sanctuaries[154] after its rectification, especially the moral catastrophe during their forum in Jeddah, which they falsely named the "Khadija Bint Khuwailid Forum" and which I wrote an address about titled *It Is Not Appropriate To Take Khadîjah bint Khuwailid's Name as a Title for Women's Liberation.* I say at this time some of the People of the Sunnah are [currently] preoccupied with derogating and cautioning against one another.[155]

I ask Allah ﷻ to grant the People of the Sunnah in every place success in clinging to the Sunnah, harmony in what is between them, cooperating upon righteousness and godliness, and discarding all of what contains division or differing between them. I ask Him, exalted is He, to grant all of the Muslims success in comprehending the religion and firmness upon the

---

Respect to the Fundamentals of Criticism, Disparagement, and Advices) written by 'Alî Ḥasan 'Abdil-Ḥamîd al-Ḥalabî and published in 1430H (2009CE), but because al-Ḥalabî himself was being demonized at the time, his book was largely disregarded and even criticized by some.

[153] *al-Bukhârî*, no. 3499, and *Muslim*, no. 188.

[154] **[t]** The cities of Mecca and Medina, i.e., Saudi Arabia.

[155] **[t]** I.e., instead of focusing on more important matters, like Westernisation, secularisation, and Feminism.

truth. And may Allah send salutations, peace, and blessings upon our Prophet Muḥammad, upon his family and his companions.

'Abdul-Muḥsin bin Ḥamad al-'Abbâd al-Badr
Wednesday, December 22, 2010CE/Muḥarram 16, 1432H